CE

A NEW HOMESTEAD in South Dakota! In the excitement of moving from Omaha to a new home, George Beine brimmed with great expectations—a stone house with four-foot walls . . . horses, pigs, and chickens . . . flower gardens . . . hunting . . . cowboys and Indians. . . . He was soon to discover, however, that the home and way of life awaiting him and his family in that treeless wind-swept land had little resemblance to what he imagined.

Continued on front flap

SHIRLEY H. COCHELL, formerly a high school teacher in Los Angeles, is now a free-lance writer. GEORGE H. BEINE was former District Manager for Metropolitan Life Insurance Company in San Francisco before his retirement.

5.95
7

LAND OF THE COYOTE

❖

LAND OF THE COYOTE

SHIRLEY HOLMES COCHELL

❖

as told by

GEORGE HOLMES BEINE

❖

THE IOWA STATE UNIVERSITY PRESS, AMES

❖

1972

❖

Universitas
BIBLIOTHECA
Ottaviensis

3 4 8 8 9 2

F
651
.B4
1972

SHIRLEY HOLMES COCHELL, a native Iowan, spent eleven years with the Los Angeles City schools as a high school instructor of English, public speaking, and social studies before turning to writing for a full-time career. During her years as a teacher, she had numerous articles published in educational journals and magazines. She has also done book reviews and evaluations of educational materials for *Scholastic Teacher* magazine and *New Educational Materials,* an annual publication.

GEORGE HOLMES BEINE, whose memories of early life on the South Dakota prairie supplied the basis for this book, is a retired insurance executive. He was district manager of areas in Montana and California for the Metropolitan Life Insurance Company before he retired from his position as manager in San Francisco.

The illustrations are taken from the pages of a turn-of-the-century Montgomery Ward catalog.

© 1972 The Iowa State University Press Ames, Iowa 50010.
All rights reserved
Composed and printed by The Iowa State University Press
First edition, 1972

Library of Congress Cataloging in Publication Data
Beine, George Holmes.
    Land of the coyote.
    1. Frontier and pioneer life—South Dakota.
I. Cochell, Shirley Holmes, 1922–   II. Title.
F636.B4   917.83′03′30924[B]   76–39612
ISBN 0-8138-0410-8

CONTENTS

❖

Home Again

Ranch Hand and Wrangler

THE COYOTE was chosen in 1949 to be the state animal of South Dakota, the setting for this story of homestead life in the early 1900s. The name "The Coyote State" is said to have originated during a horse race at a military fort in 1863 when men in the 6th Iowa Cavalry shouted as they saw a South Dakota horse outdistance their own, "Look at that 'kiote' run!"

PARTING WITH THE PAST

LAST DAY IN OMAHA

I T WAS 1907; March, to be exact. A big change was about to take place. February had been a month of planning, packing, and parting with the past. Our family prepared to leave the home I had always known, the place where I was born, the city where I had spent my boyhood. I had reached my fourteenth birthday and had graduated from the eighth grade just the month before. A white rolled scroll tied with red and white ribbons, along with my class pin of sterling silver, was carefully packed in the black valise that held my most cherished possessions. The ornately lettered diploma proclaimed not only my graduation from the Vinton Street Grammar School, a remarkable achievement, but also the end of my formal schooling. I looked upon the symbol as proudly as if it were a degree from the state university at Lincoln.

Until today there had been little time to think of the new life I would be facing. Moving preparations had kept all of us actively involved, and the initial excitement when Pa announced we were going to a homestead in South Dakota had prevailed through most of the busy days. To a household including three boys, of which I was the middle member, a South Dakota homestead was an eagerly greeted adventure. Like all boys we enjoyed a day in the country and thought the visits to our grandparents' farm near Plattsmouth were never often enough or long enough. We envisioned our farm would be the exact duplicate of Grandpa's: a stone house with walls four feet thick at the end of a mile-long lane with a group of cows looking us over as we ran up the well-maintained road. Horses, pigs, and chickens would all be there. Flower gardens, just like grandmother's, would add the right amount of orange and yellow and purple to the greens and browns dominating the scene. And, of course, there would be hunting. We would be out with our shotguns every day. This would be *our* farm! Ours to enjoy day after day, forever and ever. Even better, it was near an Indian reservation and Pa had told us about nearby cattle ranches. What could be more exciting than seeing cowboys and Indians!

Pa spoke of the homestead as though it evoked pleasant memories. When he was young, single, and without responsibilities, it had been an easy life in contrast to toiling in the coal mines of Wyoming, as he did the greater part of the year. He did no farming and had no farm machinery or animals on his land. The government required only that a homesteader spend three months of each year for five years on the land in order to receive a patent.

For the young single men and women who were just putting in time, homesteading was fun. They visited, had square dances, box socials, and moonlight hayrides, all with romantic possibilities. For those who stayed the year around, mostly poor immigrants with some large families, it was a hard life. Long cold winters with unchecked icy blasts across the flat prairies, the searing droughts in summer, prairie fires, grasshopper plagues, illness, and injuries all contributed to an ever-increasing toll among those who lacked the persistence, stamina, and most of all some cash reserve to tide them over. The land did not yield large rewards for their efforts. Selling their cabins for scrap lumber, they often departed, allowing their corner of land to return to its former state. It was not likely that we would be meeting any of the people Pa had known twenty years ago.

Pa had held his land since 1883 when what is now North and South Dakota was known as Dakota Territory. He was a pioneer, "a charter member of the community," as he liked to say. *The History of Brule County* verifies that period as the arrival time of early settlers to that area:

> In the spring of 1880 three covered wagons making their way westward stopped about forty-eight miles west of Mitchell at a spot which was to become known as Kimball. By 1883 the land had been thrown open, homesteaders had begun to arrive, and Kimball was organized as a village. The 1880's were years of change and excitement in that part of the Territory. It was here that the last of the big buffalo hunts took place. Plains Indians were being herded

into reservations extending in a line from Canada to Nebraska. Indian Wars continued on, ending only shortly after Sitting Bull, the great Sioux Indian Chief, was killed on December 15, 1890.

By 1905, land was selling for twenty dollars an acre, but Pa had always said that he would never sell, that he would hold it to return to in case of emergency. It seemed as though that emergency had now arrived.

Last fall, he had gone up to look things over and, if possible, make a trade for a place "with improvements." He found such a place, three quarter sections in a row, thirty miles to the northwest, adjacent to the Crow Indian Reservation. Pa's description of it as having a house, barn, pens, corncribs, a fenced pasture, an artesian well, and seventy acres under plow—not to mention a large mortgage—inflated our imaginations and our expectations.

And now the last day had arrived. Tomorrow we would be leaving and very little was left to do. I sat alone to think: *If we were only leaving for a long vacation, with the good feeling that we would come back soon.* But that wasn't the case. Unhappily, I recalled all that had gone before, knowing that those childhood pleasures I had known were never to return.

Through my window I could see the woods and rolling hills only a few hundred yards from our house. Across the dirt street was a creek. No law existed to prevent our cutting down trees, which we enjoyed doing to hear them crash. It was hard work however and this had precluded their wholesale destruction. We built fires of the wood, especially in winter after we enjoyed our slides down the snow-covered hills.

What happy hours we had spent there! I thought of the squirrels and cottontail rabbits playing in the woods and the quail that startled us when they whizzed away close to our feet. We had watched the oriole build her hanging basket nest and then climbed up to peek in at the eggs. Later after they hatched we watched the mother bird feed the tiny creatures huge globs of angleworms and grubs and waited anxious and breathless as she taught them to fly. We caught butterflies to examine more closely the beauty of their wings. We learned the names of all the wild flowers and gloried whenever we found the more beautiful and rare ones, as the johnny-jump-up, dutchman's breeches, jack-in-the-pulpit, and lady's slipper.

As we became older, the woods grew to be ours more and

more. We discovered our huge natural playground could be the center of our universe. Anything we wanted it to be it became. It was at times a huge Indian battleground infested with Indians. We fought with spears, bows and arrows, and guns we had made of sticks. In the fall we heaped huge piles of dry leaves for many days, and on a quiet, very dark night we created a tremendous bonfire.

On summer Sundays various clubs and lodges invaded our sacred hollows and held picnics. These fun-loving intruders were all "foreigners:" Germans, Danes, and Bohemians. We were intrigued with and delighted by their accents and customs. They had barrels of beer and always music and folk dancing. We sat on a hill, unobserved, to watch them in their colorful costumes until after dark and past bedtime. Eagerly we waited for early morning when we could search for things that had been left. We often found some beer in the kegs; it was very good.

Once we made a swing of one long rope tied to a high branch of a large sturdy oak standing halfway up a steep slope. This enabled us, seated on the slender piece of wood at the end of the rope, to start at the very top of the hill and swing down over the deep canyon. It was very frightening, and we hung on for dear life.

The McGrath kids herded their cows in one flattened hollow; certainly no place to hold a picnic but we played ball there. Between games, we took turns at "skinning" the infield. It was hard work, but after that the cow pies were confined to the outfield and it was worth it.

Deciding to take a last look at our neighborhood and to say good-bye to a few friends, I walked up to Twentieth Street. I was glad the firemen were sitting around the station; they were the ones I wanted to see. We passed the firehouse each day to and from school. The firemen played marbles, spun tops with us, and settled disputes. We liked the beautiful friendly horses and watched them prance while being exercised each day. We hooked rides on the firewagons.

I would always remember the cold winter day Bennett's five-story department store burned to the ground. The fire lasted throughout the day and night. By morning the ice-covered building collapsed. Three of our friends died and the firehouse bore black bunting for days. I remembered the great sorrow shared by all of us.

From the fire station I walked down to the river bottom

6 ❖

where we used to pick chokecherries, wild grapes, and red haws and gather hickory nuts. I wandered down to the hazelnut thickets where we had found the cleverly concealed cave which had turned out to be a hiding place for robbers' loot. We were glad the robbers weren't there when we found it! I remembered thinking about it for days and having bad dreams at night.

The people down by the river were mostly Indians, blacks, or bad whites living in hovels made of flotsam and tin. We were afraid of them, but our curiosity impelled us to go among them. Some of them had pigs which lived on nuts and acorns. I turned back before reaching their area because none of us ever went there unless he had a slingshot and the old single shot .22 rifle. Only one man ever bothered us, and he stopped when we aimed the .22 around kind of carelessly.

I walked downtown to get my evening papers. A lot of kids were there I knew, but I didn't say good-bye to them. I sold only twelve papers—there was not much news that day—and gave the other thirteen to Joe Maleziva beause he was little and poor and always shivered and had a cold.

When I got home the last things had been packed in barrels and boxes. The house no longer resembled our home. Pa was mad about something. He got mad a lot but was worse lately. I guess things were not going very well, or maybe he had a toothache, because he was red in the face and he scolded something fierce.

We had supper late, but I didn't care because it wasn't a very good supper, just macaroni boiled in milk, with tea and a cookie. The macaroni tasted like slippery wet flour.

Supper was glumly quiet because no one talked when Pa was mad. All we heard was the slurping of the milky macaroni, an awful sound when everything else is so quiet. I was going to have an apple, but it was gone when I went to my hiding place to get it. Places to hide things in our small house were few, and my younger brother always found anything like an apple. I usually ate them right away as he did his, and I wished I had eaten this one. There wasn't anything to do so I went to bed right away, and I cried a little.

Thoughts of the pleasures to come were now relegated to the joys we were to know no more, most of all those Saturday nights free of parental supervision. Rather than be disturbed at four or four-thirty Sunday mornings when we had to get up to walk several miles to downtown Omaha to get our Sunday papers, Pa had agreed that we could go down the night before. We would sleep on large stuffing tables where sections of the paper were assembled in the basement of the "Bee" building. The tables were hard, the kids were noisily disagreeable, and we were quite aware that sleep was out of the question. Little did Pa and Ma know that our customary procedure was first to get some Virginia cheroots or a couple of "Cremo" cigars, two for five cents, then to head for the Orpheum Theater where for ten cents each we could go up to what was called "nigger heaven" (we didn't recognize the slur then). The seats were hard benches and so far from the stage that our heads almost touched the ceiling. When the kids got too rowdy and persisted in throwing objects down on the audience below, this area was prohibited to us. We then began patronizing some of the smaller playhouses, where we enjoyed such melodramas as "Her First False Step" and "The Cuban Spy," or an amateur vaudeville house from which we were soon barred. One house showed "moving pictures," which were flickery silents, of ten-minute duration. We thought they were indeed sensational.

After the show we prowled around following the older boys. They participated in such pranks as tying some livery stable buggies in tandem and coasting them down a steep hill, raising havoc with the jugs at a distillery, and going into an all night eating place where at a given moment one boy pulled the light switch. By the time the lights were on again the boys were gone, and so were apples, oranges, and doughnuts.

We would also miss the joy of having our own money to spend as we wished. Pa taught us thrift to excess—he had a phobia about it—but it was with our earnings, our money! Each night he would hold his hand out. "Come," he would say while rubbing his thumb and forefinger together, "I'll save it for you," and into his deep pocket it would go, never to be seen again. But we always held some out, and there were days when "extras" came out and we could hold out a lot of money. The Cudahy boy's kidnap broke new stories every day: the notes tossed by a phantom rider, finally the capture of Pat Crowe, the trial, and other developments. It was the biggest story ever in Omaha. Other events meriting extras were the tragic Bennett's Store fire, the San Francisco earthquake with pictures, and the Sunday Pope Leo died. Daily papers cost us one-half cent and sold for one cent; extras cost two cents, sold for five cents. Pa could never estimate our take on those days. Our hiding place in an old oak was never quite out of a few pieces of silver. Besides the shows and the cheroots, we bought pies (raisin mostly) for five cents each at the pie factory, cream puffs, pigs feet, dill pickles, a cantaloupe or watermelon, warm fresh pastries, and sometimes a bottle of milk; we were always hungry. Money for these joys would be a great loss to us.

There might be some other losses, too; happily not so distasteful. No longer after a sleepless Saturday night downtown followed by walking the streets selling Sunday papers would we have to rush through our breakfast, dress up, and walk more blocks to St. Patrick's Church. There on a hard first row bench we sat under the watchful eyes of Father John Smith, who we thought disliked kids and scolded the congregation. It was ten o'clock Mass; but at twelve noon and often later the good Father was still scolding in his thick Irish brogue, pausing only long enough to wipe his lips occasionally. He would look straight down at us while voicing his opinion of a boy who would part his hair in the middle and be "the fool at one end of a cigarette, a light at the other." At Easter time his attention focused on "women coming to church to show off their hats and other clothes."

On a number of special Sundays money was collected for specific purposes: the "winter's coal," "a new roof," "Peter's Pence," and always Easter and Christmas. On these days he customarily read the names of all contributors and the amount each had donated. He chanted the list in a singsong similar to the Litany of the Saints. Most of the congregation were poor Irish, but among the more affluent were the Minogues, two brothers who, with their respective families, lived in huge Victorian houses on a hill overlooking the Missouri River. Not content with one "Mr. and Mrs." contribution, these families divided their amount among themselves and their children. With the four parents and thirteen youngsters in one family and eleven in the other, a total of twenty-eight Minogue names and each one's contribution of one dollar was read. At one time, I had been sentenced to pump the organ along with several other boys for some infraction, which in my case was having fallen asleep during several especially long sermons. Other folks were no doubt irked as I was when Father droned on and on with the list of givers. When he began reading the list of Minogues, I began to reply almost inaudibly, "Pray for us" . . . "Pray for us" . . . "Pray for us." Those near me first began to laugh and then joined in, softly at first but more boldly as it went on. Our responses came to an abrupt stop however when Father Smith dispatched one of the nuns who, though she indicated she thought it was funny, had to inform me I was to go immediately to the sanctum sanctorum where I was to await Father Smith. I don't remember all he said but I think I was excommunicated. After that I went to the German Catholic church for confessions and communions. As a result, the German priests called at our house for a contribution. The first time there were only two, but treated royally with cigars and beer, they came again and again, bringing several of the brothers with them. Their German guttural and laughter grew louder into the wee hours, and there was little chance for sleep in our tiny house. Morning found the place reeking with the stale odor of cigar smoke and beer. Ma counted the cigar butts and empty bottles. "So many dead butts and bottles," she muttered to me as she counted them, "and it's all your fault!" My quip, "They received extreme unction at least," did not help matters. Pa made no comment, as he no doubt welcomed the excuse to imbibe. What better excuse would he ever have?

Obviously, our Sundays were something we did not look forward to with any degree of pleasure, for after church there was the long walk home, a hasty noon dinner, and back to the church for Sunday school for another hour and a half. Recitation of the catechism was word for word, especially by those who did not attend St. Patrick's parochial school. For me learning anything by heart, especially if I didn't understand it, came hard.

I recalled Pa saying there was no church or Sunday school within miles of the homestead. Yes, there were some things I would be willing to give up. I dried my eyes and went to sleep.

HOMESTEAD BOUND

THE MIDWEST can be very bleak in March, with strong cold winds blowing from the river across frozen bare ground through naked tree limbs under a dark, threatening sky. It was good to be on a train headed north from Omaha. I thought of Pa, still at home, and the busy day that lay ahead of him after putting Ma and us kids on the train.

All the packing had been completed before we left. Household goods were boxed and barreled and our chickens crated. With the aid of the Carpenter Drayage Company, the firm that he had employed for years to haul his flour from the boxcars to the little warehouse on our home lot, Pa was to haul everything to a chartered boxcar on a siding. Into this boxcar were to go our household belongings, the chickens, his horses and wagon, feed, hay, a mattress, and a supply of food. Pa would ride along to care for the horses and chickens. He would "take up residence" in his freight car that day and await its being added to a train.

As our train neared the railroad junction at Mankato in southwestern Minnesota, we gathered our valise and bundles and prepared to wait for the train west. As we entered the station, Nick checked to be sure he still had the alarm clock in his pocket and we had all our belongings. There we sat on that chilly spring day: Nick, 16; myself, George, 14; Eddie, 11; Agnes, 6; and our mother. Agnes, as the youngest family member and the only girl, was usually overlooked by my brothers and me when thinking of family activities. In her little blue bonnet and matching coat, Agnes sat bewildered and apprehensive on the hard wooden high-backed bench, close to Ma, as she had in the train coach. She said little but observed much through her large blue eyes. Her feet dangled about six inches above the floor, and she sat very straight.

Suddenly the station door opened and a woman with four children about our ages entered. In contrast to our well-groomed hair, shined shoes, long black ribbed stockings, knee pants, and sailor hats, these kids wore faded patched overalls, patched shoes, and no hats. Their unkempt hair hung long on all sides, over their necks, and down their foreheads. When we approached in an attempt toward friendship they scattered like frightened animals.

Their more garrulous mother had deposited her bundles and was already engaged in animated conversation with our usually shy mother. This woman's dress was old and faded, her shoes unpolished and ill fitting, her coat threadbare, and her hat looked as though a horse had stepped on it. Her face was leathered and her hands calloused. In contrast, our mother looked exceptionally beautiful. She was wearing her only good outfit, which she so seldom wore I remember it in detail. Her shirred taffeta pink shirtwaist had a high lace trimmed collar stayed with whalebone, and a little gold watch pin set it off. Her hat, with her hair in pompadour beneath it, was trimmed with birds' wings, as was the mode of the day. Her polished high buttoned shoes were scarcely visible beneath a full charcoal black skirt.

It gave me a feeling of relief to see this incongruous group soon board a train going east, the opposite direction to our destination. When I returned to join my mother on the bench, she was in tears. As first, all she would say was that those people had had a hard time and she had given the woman some money to buy milk for the children. Then she said they had lived for seven years on a homestead not far from where we were going.

Later Ma said, "She was apologetic about her appearance and that of the children. She said that she looked like me when they came out. I wonder what Pa is getting us into."

When we arrived in Kimball, it was already dark. The little town was very quiet and the street deserted. A few kerosene lamps threw dim lights from windows. We had eaten little food on the trip and, accustomed to having all of our meals at home, looked forward to eating out for a few days. The first meal was a disappointment. We had dinner at the Kimball House where we were the only ones in the dining room, and we had warmed over food. Evening did not improve our situation since the Kimball House had no lobby, and we sat in our room with nothing to do before going to bed.

Days passed slowly while we waited for Pa to join us. It was several days before his boxcar became part of a train to the railroad junction in Minnesota. He spent another two days there on a siding until it joined a train west. There was no beauty in Kimball to begin with, and as the days passed we became more aware of its ugliness. Save for a few remaining dirty, sooty drifts, the snow had melted leaving the dregs of winter. Horses had pawed holes in front of hitching racks to form mounds of dirt and horse manure. Windblown dust sifted into the stores and over the merchandise. Weeds grew along the wooden sidewalks, and there were no trees. The sweet alkali water caused us to make frequent visits to the community outhouse in the center of a vacant lot down by the depot.

We boys spent much of our time down at the railroad yards watching the trains and the loading and unloading of cattle. Agnes stayed close to the hotel. The days were most difficult for Ma however. She had never before known a moment when she was unoccupied, and for her the waiting and idleness were depressing. She was certain something calamitous was causing the delay.

Arriving in Kimball, Pa sent a man to the Kimball House immediately to let us know that his boxcar with all our household possessions was being shunted to a siding. His appearance after days of traveling in that manner hardly made him presentable for visiting the hotel and notifying us himself. Besides, the pressure of duties required that he stay at the boxcar and supervise the unloading so that we could proceed to the homestead that day.

We rushed down to greet Pa and found quite a commotion. Horses, frightened by clouds of exhaust steam and the ringing of engine bells, were pitching and squealing. Only the two men in charge of them seemed unperturbed.

Pa called to us and introduced them as "Jupe" Tegethoff and Dan Barth. Jupe, the older of the two, was an old friend who had relinquished his homestead near Pa's and had taken up a better one near the Rosebud Agency. At the time Pa was in South Dakota in the fall making the trade of his unimproved homestead for the one with a house and farm buildings, he called on Jupe to make necessary arrangements for transporting our goods to the farm. Jupe had offered to buy horses that were readily available in that locale. One look at those frisky broncos told us they were nothing more than partially tamed mustangs. Jupe had agreed to deliver the horses, buy the wagons, and help us haul our worldly goods from the boxcar to the homestead. He was a smelly character, squat, deep chested, and rough; but he laughed easily.

Dan was young, no more than thirty. His clothes, in contrast, were clean, in spite of the fact that he and Jupe had slept in one of the wagons while waiting for Pa's train to arrive. He wore a gun strapped to his hip, "for target shooting," he assured us.

By the time the wagons were loaded the sun was low in the west and we were in a gay mood. Starting out that near to dusk seemed all right since the distance to the homestead was not great, about seventeen miles. The men passed a bottle between them and attempted to join us kids in songs we had learned in school. Dan told stories and delighted us by shooting at prairie chickens on the wing. The time passed swiftly at first.

As it grew dusk we became tired; there was nothing to see.

It was as though we were on an ocean of grass. It was totally dark by the time we reached the point where we had to leave the road and travel at an angle across country. Jupe assured us there was a trail, but we strongly doubted we were on it. Looking as best we could, we told him we could not see it. "Those lead horses can see it," he claimed. "They never get lost."

We ate some fresh bread and sausage and drank some milk; everything tasted so good. The men had more whiskey, and we could smell the smoke from their cigars and see the lights from them glow in the dark.

Except for the horses breathing and the pounding of their hoofs, all was quiet—or so it seemed. Eddie was tired and complained of the cold until Pa took him over near him and wrapped him in a blanket. Agnes cried, frightened and insecure in the dark.

Suddenly, Jupe, who was in the lead, cried, "Whoa!"

"We should be there already," he shouted. "You stay here. I'll make a circle and find the trail."

So! We had not been on the trail! The sound of his wagon faded away, and we were alone. Lost out there in the dark!

Time dragged on, and Ma whispered, out of Pa's hearing, that she was sure that Jupe was lost "away out there somewhere!" How could he find us? No one had thought to put a lantern in our wagon. How long had he been gone? Pa had a watch but didn't tell us the time. The faraway sound of a coyote barking added to the eeriness. Many Indians claim to understand the coyote's language, and as the sound changed to a quavering howl I wished that we, too, knew what that call meant.

It must have been at least an hour before we heard Jupe's wagon again and at the same moment his shout, "Over this way! Follow me!"

We followed, down into draws, up slopes, over rocks that threatened to snap a wheel or a horse's leg, never knowing when one of our wagons might tip over and land in a gully. It must have been another hour before we knew we were once again on the trail, with no rocks and fewer bumps.

The night was so dark we could scarcely see the outline of a building when Jupe shouted, "Here we are!"

"What's that noise?" we asked. "It sounded like steam blowing off." It was an odd sound to hear in the middle of a prairie.

"Artesian well," explained Jupe, as he began to give orders.

"Over here! Look alive there and give me a hand with this."

He deserved some credit for thinking to put everything we would need first into one wagon: lanterns, kerosene, the stove, and food. After the horses were stabled and fed, we prepared to set things up for housekeeping.

Approaching the house, we saw Ma sitting outside on a box, a lantern in her hand, sobbing.

"There are snakes in there," she cried.

Sure enough there were—along the walls, in the corners, peering out of coiled bodies, beady eyes glistening, tongues flicking, hissing when one of us came near. From room to room we went disposing of them, feeling safe on Jupe's assurance they weren't rattlers.

"Only water snakes," he said. "Maybe a couple of gopher snakes."

After a good meal of thick bacon, boiled potatoes with milk gravy, and canned peaches, we set up the beds and slept, but not for long! There was a rumbling. We lit a match; the noise stopped. Another five, ten, fifteen minutes, and there it was again, on and on, through the night. I wished Jupe and Dan had not decided to sleep in the barn.

Daylight came at last, and when Jupe appeared soon after feeding the horses, we told him about the noise.

"Oh, only rats," Jupe answered. "We brought in some corn for the kitchen stove last night. They prob'ly dragged it across the floor. See, here," he pointed, "they left a few ears out there, too big to get into the hole."

After that, we decided to keep the corn in a box, out-of-doors!

EXPLORING

IN THE DAYLIGHT HOURS we had a chance to look around our homestead. Not only was it not the farm of our dreams, but it also lacked any resemblance to any farm of our imaginations.

Only brief investigation of our oddly shaped one-story house was needed to conclude it was a series of lean-tos added to a central cabin. The house had been built with the aid of neither plumb nor square, so dust, snow, and winds had free access. Lean-tos had been added on all four sides of the center room, which apparently had been the original cabin. Two others were added at corners, making a total of seven rooms. The house was said to have been the home of the Henzliks, who added to its size as their family continually increased. In the fourteen years they homesteaded this land they had thirteen children.

We put our only heating stove in the center room which, because of the lean-tos, had four doors and no windows. Each of the six added rooms had one window; each rattled with the wind and, we learned later, allowed enough snow to sift through to reach sill high.

The rough pine board floors had occasional cracks large enough to simplify our sweeping and make a dustpan totally unnecessary. Moreover, field stones had been used for the foundation, and no one had thought of banking its perimeter with dirt to prevent the cold prairie winds from coming up through the knotholes and the cracks in the floor.

It was a simply constructed house, with no closets and no cupboards. Each room had been held to the bare minimum of four walls. Of course there were no utilities. When asked last night where the outhouse might be, Jupe informed us that outhouses are unnecessary when one has a barn and, besides, the first high wind would carry it away. No doubt he was right about that last part, for we soon discovered there had once been an outhouse. It now lay against the corral and was beyond repair.

The farm consisted only of weatherbeaten buildings that had never known a coat of paint. All leaned crazily to the lee of prevailing winds, and mounds of earth created by windblown dust stood out sharply at each northeast corner. Warped boards rattled with the breeze. Doors hung loose on their broken hinges. The roof of the corncrib lay shattered by the wind. Everywhere we looked we were greeted by work to be done.

As we approached the barn, I recalled learning that "the barn is always considered the farmer's pride and the showplace of his farm." This one was long and high in the center for hay, with lean-tos at each side as if to hold it up. It contained rows of mangers and horses' stalls. Manure, still frozen, had piled up over the years to a height that compelled the horses to crouch in order to enter the barn, and in their stalls the accumulations caused their hind feet to be so much higher than their forefeet they stood on a slope.

The cow barn defied inspection. Oozing with the runoff of melting snow, it was knee deep in evil smelling muck.

There were many indications our farm had been unoccupied for some time. Parts of an old wagon and scraps of rusted farm machinery lay scattered among the flourishing weeds everywhere. Corral posts tilted this way and that. Fences were a mass of rusty twisted barbed wire and broken posts still holding back intermittent accumulations of tumbleweeds.

The artesian well poured a constant stream of warm iron-and-sulphur-tasting water from a two-inch pipe. It was at the top of a slight rise which made it possible to point the flow in any direction. At this time, however, it was in a mire around which lay the remains of dead animals. A number of dead cattle in various stages of decomposition also lay around the water hole below the barn.

"Better you should drag those carcasses down the draw while they are still froze," admonished Jupe, "or you will have a hell of a stink."

Other than some of the lean-tos which were part of the house, the granary appeared to have been the most recent construction and was in surprisingly good repair. In one dark corner was a heap of small yellow seeds or grain of some sort, which Jupe, in answer to Pa's question, replied were turnip seeds.

"Well, we don't need that many turnips," said Pa.

After lunch, we hitched a team to go explore the neighborhood. Ma and Agnes did not go with us since they were busy unpacking and arranging our possessions. Ma preferred to have the house in order before venturing out into the community. Jupe, Dan, Pa, and we three boys took a turn up around the one-room schoolhouse which Pa informed us was on the far corner of our land. The scholars (we counted eight) rushed to the windows to get a view of the unusual sight of our painted wagon bearing the legend, "Frank Beine, Agent, Wahoo Flour Mills," in large gold lettering. Anxious to see our post office and general store, we drove on to Vega, choosing our route carefully, going first along the section lines, then out and down a hill to bypass a washed out culvert, crossing again to the other side to ford a spring freshet formed by the melting snow. The horses slid and strained for footing.

Vega itself was on flat ground at a crossroad. The town consisted of only two buildings, both two stories, and on opposite sides of the road. No signboards indicated the kind of business conducted in either place. We entered first the one containing the post office which, at first glance, was quite a contrast to the standard one we had used in Omaha. The Vega Post Office consisted mainly of two boxes, one for "incoming" and one for "outgoing" mail. To our surprise, Jim Havlik, the taciturn proprietor, handed us our mail without our asking, and were we glad to see the bundle of Omaha newspapers!

"Now we'll have something to read tonight," I told Nick excitedly.

Ma and all of us were anxious to know what had been happening in Omaha since we left.

Looking around the main room, we noted Jim stocked a few articles of canned goods and other supplies, described best as "a few of these and one of that," in general disarray. In a small corner room, off to the right, we could see a dust-covered pool table, a card table, and a few battered wooden chairs. Hair on the floor indicated that the cowboy who doubled as the town barber on Saturday nights had neglected the broom in his rush to get away early. Small dirty windows allowed only meager light.

On the floor above was the dance hall, entered only by an outside stairway. Crude benches lined the walls. At the far end was an upright piano with the ivory missing from several keys. The strong daylight brought out all the shabby features of the large cold room.

While we were making our inspections, Jim had taken the three men out to the rear to a blacksmith shop of sorts in which there was a small bar. There he handed out the bottle—to *pour* a drink for another would have bordered on insult. Jim enjoyed telling about the only time he had ever been asked whether he held a license to dispense liquor.

"What the matter, you blind or something? It's in plain sight," he claimed to have replied, pointing to the 30-30 on the wall behind him. "Mister," he had added, pointing north, "the road runs that way."

Jim declared he had made no threat. "I just answered the man's question; even showed him which direction the road runs, as any good neighbor should. He left hastily, without a word." Jim smiled triumphantly as he recalled the stranger's departure.

The other building, across the section road, stood on the corner of the Fousek farm. It appeared to be just a two-story house, but we knew it had to be the general store. After crossing the railless porch, we found the entire lower floor was stocked with merchandise in fairly neat display. We went in to meet the owner and browse. The prices seemed high until one recalled that everything had to be brought out from the railroad at Pukwana by horse drawn freight. We learned too that no money changed hands at the time of purchase, and for some time afterward. Butter, eggs, and cream the farmer brought to the store were credited against the amount due, and the rest of his bill was added to his account in the ledger "to be paid when the crops are in."

Fousek also provided a much-needed service for the farmers, a small creamery where he employed a butter maker who boarded with the Fouseks. Chatting briefly with the young man, we learned that without cooling facilities farm butter was often rancid and cream became sour and flyblown and sometimes even contained a rodent or two. He assured us he did an excellent job of remaking the offensive butter into a palatable spread.

However, as we became acquainted with some more talkative members of the community, we learned there had been only one butter maker who was worthy of the title. Unfortunately, since the duty of bringing cream and eggs to the village customarily fell to the daughters, that handsome young agriculture college graduate was only too happy to assist the girls in unloading the heavy cans and eagerly seized his opportunity to become better acquainted with many of them. He basked in popularity until a few of the girls compared notes and found his secret promises had been generously extended to all. He left abruptly for parts unknown, most likely Canada.

Folks for miles around suffered after he was gone since no one could be found to fill the modest-income butter maker's job. Several had tried it but each failed, and the present one would also. Butter and cream had to be hauled to Pukwana or it would grow rancid. Some was used in cooking; much of it spoiled. Once when the former butter maker's name came up, Fousek was reported to have said, "He was a great butter maker. I wish his work had been his only asset."

We met the younger Fousek children and learned that the oldest son who had been sent to college in Iowa City was editor of the Pukwana *Press*.

The store was referred to as "V. Fousek's." V. Fousek—I never learned what the "V." stood for—was the best educated of anyone around. He had gained political offices and positions on the school board and on the road commission. For the price of the certificate, he was ordained as a minister so that he performed marriage ceremonies and read from the Bible at funerals.

His marriages were performed on the road, either on his side in Buffalo County or on the other side, Brule County, depending on which county had issued the license. Funeral services were performed at the gravesite in a small weedy plot enclosed by rusted barbed wire in the pasture behind the store.

Looking at the "cemetery" that day, we did not realize how much more forlorn and desolate it could appear at the time of a burial. The following winter we happened to come to town just as a funeral was about to take place. Since those were years of customary ostentatious display at funerals (and we had witnessed several of this kind in Omaha), it seemed pitiful to see a spring wagon carrying a pine box to this resting place. There were no flowers and no song except the wail of a chill wind. Only a handful of mourners, possibly six, stood shivering and muffled to the eyes. The mound of earth beside the grave seemed all too small, the words too few. Moreover, we learned that it was always necessary for the bereaved or a friend to dig the grave.

It seemed to us that all drinking took place only on the other side of the road, at Jim Havlik's. Later we learned it had not always been so. Every wedding used to call for "a private celebration," every funeral "a private wake," and every business day was rated "good" or "poor" to determine the type of drink required. Eventually, Fousek did not need the incentive of weddings or funerals nor justified reasons "to tie on a bun." His "square face" of bitters each day served to keep him in a state of perpetual inebriation. At that point his family became concerned enough to try anything. He was sent off to Iowa to undergo the new and expensive "gold cure" injections. Everyone had said, "Of course, it won't work," but miraculously it did and Fousek never drank again.

LEFT TO SURVIVE

THE MORNING AFTER our visit to Vega I was awakened by
Jupe's boisterous singing as he led his team to water.

"Hi li, hi low, ghets immer, ghets schlimmer, ghets
so." He repeated the words over and over on tunes that varied
from a Bavarian tenor to a Plattdeutsch guttural.

His reason for bursting into song was to arouse us "late sleep-
ers," for he was leaving that day and obviously wanted breakfast
which, when provided, both he and Dan downed with gusto.
Ahead of them lay a trek of 120 miles to the Rosebud Agency.

Ma had really outdone herself, with hot cereal, thick slices of
bacon, mounds of fried potatoes, and a seemingly endless supply
of scrambled eggs and toasted bread. Pots of steaming coffee
regularly appeared and disappeared. It was truly a last meal for
the trail.

"We don't get more meals like this for three, four days," Jupe
managed between mouthfuls. "Take 'bout that long to get back,"
he continued. "We haff bread and wusht" (I knew he was talking
about some kind of meat, probably knackwurst). "And coffee,"
he added. "Ya, we build fire and make coffee."

The two men wasted no time after breakfast. They faced a
long, hard trip and were anxious to be on their way. Pa gave
Jupe a check, a supply of food, a bottle of Old Crow, and we
said our good-byes.

Jupe was hunched over on the spring seat of his wagon. Sun-
bleached hair, sticking out every which way from under a well-
worn hat that had absorbed much sweat and dust, added to his
careless appearance. Broad suspenders, which he called galluses,
were caked with the soil of toil. His socks drooped over his sturdy
shoes. Behind him, the provisions were neatly stacked and covered
with canvas.

Dan, "the horseman," looked the part. Sitting straight without effort, his long slim back looked even more slender as his
dungarees hung low with the weight of cartridge belt, gun, and
holster. His hat, tilted back, revealed strands of fair hair framing

blue eyes that seemed ever on the alert for new adventure or whatever might come his way.

Pa, neat and clean—too neat and too clean, with hands too soft for the setting—completed the scene, a study in contrast.

"You will make out just fine, Franz," Jupe assured Pa, using Pa's real name, the one which appears on the records of his original homestead.

The two hired men were leaving in high spirits, taking with them, I thought, the best team and the best wagon. As he slapped his horses to a trot, Jupe felt the pocket in which he had Pa's check for $580. Of course it was too much, but that was the price they had asked and Pa had agreed to. Had we been experienced, we could have bought tried-and-true plow horses for less. What we needed less than anything was to be left with half-wild unpredictable horses which would expend their energy in such nervous gyrations as to exhaust both themselves and their driver with little good results. In defense of Jupe and Dan, however, it should be said that no man who risks his neck and takes chances at serious injury in taming horses ever believes he gets enough money for them.

Seeing them leave, Ma expressed her relief: "Those men made extra work. They leered, and Jupe was dirty. I don't trust him."

Her suspicions were probably justified. Perhaps, however, they thought they had done us a real favor and had taken it for granted those were really good horses. But they were their kind of horses, broncos, not the type for city boys. The horses proved dangerous and very difficult to handle. Certainly Dan and Jupe could not be expected to know some of the problems those animals generated. One horse, a nervous bay, turned out to be a runaway. At least once he ran away with everything he was hitched to, breaking equipment and injuring himself and the other half of the team. That horse should have been sold. In keeping him, Pa exposed us all to serious consequences. Another horse ran himself into a sweat one very cold day, broke out of the barn, caught pneumonia, and died. Still another got caught in barbed wire and sawed the tendon of one foot; he eventually recovered but continued lame.

We never saw or heard from Jupe or his man Dan again. It was excusable perhaps, because Jupe had never learned to read or write. He had to sign his name with an "X" on the receipt Pa had prepared for him.

As Jupe's wagon disappeared out of sight over the first rise in the prairie, we turned slowly toward the house.

"Now we have to go to work," said Pa.

We did not have to search for the things to do; the question was, "Where to start?" Much needed to be done, and the evidence was everywhere: rotting carcasses, broken fences, loose clapboards, rubble, weeds, and manure. An "improved" farm, perhaps, but not a going one. We needed farm machinery, field equipment, repair and maintenance supplies, cows, pigs—the whole outlay. We didn't even own a dog. Our livestock consisted of horses that would spook at the drop of a hat and a crate of chickens brought along from Omaha in the boxcar.

We would soon realize what tenderfeet we were. We had no knowledge or experience to fall back on as we tried to organize the farm and solve ensuing problems. What farm implements were required? How would we prepare the soil? What would we plant? And when? Where would we get the seed? Our survival seemed to depend on watching the neighbors and asking questions.

 APPRENTICE FARMERS

MA ENTERED INTO the new enterprise with the determination of her pioneer parents. She was ready to accomplish in Dakota the productive successful farming that would do credit to her Nebraska forebears. Her immediate contribution was our "work clothes," which she had somehow managed to make, without our knowing, during the final months in Omaha. They were overalls, light blue with rows of white stars; I had never seen any overalls so thin or so skimpy, suitable only for comic opera. Our straw hats, purchased in an Omaha department store, proved so light they folded in the wind and sailed away with the tumbleweeds. When we retrieved them, Ma attached garter elastic to fit under our chins.

The first week produced several near-catastrophes that brought us to a quick realization of innumerable facets in general farming and the raising of farm animals. We now could understand why most of the homesteaders, lacking experience, were not able to overcome the odds already weighted against them by the elements.

Pa had brought several sacks of left-over oats from his boxcar. We poured them on the first day into an empty packing box about four feet square. It was no great surprise or of any concern when the next day we discovered it was occupied by two or three rats that had with considerable diligence succeeded in gnawing a hole at one corner scarcely large enough for them to crawl through. But on the following morning when we opened the lid we were surprised by a stream of rats that bubbled over on all sides, over our feet, and everywhere. We simultaneously jumped and dropped the lid. We did not need another look to convince us there were as many as could fill the entire space not taken up by the oats.

Our minds raced. What to do about it? We were in a dilemma. How does one get rid of so many vile rodents? How would we dispose of them? How many there were we could never guess. We had to do something. We would try anything.

We hit on the gunnysack idea. Holding the sack over the now-enlarged hole made by the rats, one of us pounded on the sides of the box. Success was immediate; the sack began to fill. It became heavier and heavier. When it was about three-quarters full they quit coming. That part of our task had been accomplished—we had them. Now, what to do with them?

Of several ideas that came to mind, we decided the lesser of the evils was to club them while they were in the sack, dig a large hole, and bury them.

It was a repugnant but necessary job. We were tired but elated when it was over. Our satisfaction proved to be short-lived, however, for the next day we had to go through it again, and the next day, and the next, and several after. Finally the number of rats began to taper off until one day, happily, there were none.

Ed and Agnes were trudging off each day to school carrying their Karo-Syrup-can lunch pail filled with day-old bread, cold fat pork, and prunes. Pa was negotiating for a couple cows and some sows with farrow. Ma set some hens on duck and turkey eggs and planned to churn butter which we would trade at Vega for groceries and clothes.

Most of the cleanup task was assigned to Nick and me. After only one-half day of trying to load manure with a shovel and a hay fork, our too-soft hands bore painful blisters where calluses would eventually be. When the blisters broke they burned like fire. Wind chapped our lips and seared our tender faces. Muscles unaccustomed to physical effort cried out in pain and anger. Pa sought solace in a cigar and a bottle of beer. For us there was no relief from our discomfort.

A day or two after Jupe and Dan had left, Pa correctly decided that young horses stabled too long become fractious and unmanageable. He turned them into the pasture where in high spirits they kicked and squealed with tails flying until, finding a low place in the fence, they jumped over and took off in the direction from whence they had come. We could only stand in despair, watching them race on until they were swallowed by the horizon. They were born to run, and with nothing out there but space, catching them was out of the question.

Days passed. We wondered if this was a foreboding of troubles we should continue to expect; the thought was disheartening. We began to inquire about the possibility of buying some cheap old horses, the only kind we could now afford, anything that would tide us over for a year or two.

One morning a man drove up in a fine rig. We surely couldn't afford anything he might have to sell! He had a rangy black team, a shiny harness set off with red and white spreaders, a new top buggy with yellow wheels that glistened in the sunlight. His personal appearance was even more striking. He had a fawn-colored cattleman's hat with gloves to match. A polished cowman's boot with curlicue stitching rested easily on the dashboard.

"Hello," he greeted Pa, as our father came out onto the porch. "I'm Charley Saunders. Did you have some horses stray?"

I shall never forget those words in that deep nasal drawl with just a tinge of English accent. How out of his environment I thought this man of apparent wealth, culture, and refinement looked as he sat in our humble kitchen. Its white bare walls had cracked plaster and there were no furnishings other than the cheapest of chairs and kitchen table. He accepted Pa's offer of a drink and a cigar, after which he left as abruptly as he had come.

"Now you don't owe me a thing," he said in parting. "I'll have my men bring them in a day or two. Glad to do it."

The very next evening two fine-looking young cowboys not over seventeen years of age headed our horses, looking fit, into the barn where they haltered them and prepared to leave.

"About sixteen miles due west; the river stopped them—the Missouri is high this time of year," the garrulous one replied to our question.

I wanted to meet Mr. Saunders again, because I thought there must be quite a story behind his knowing about those horses. Although I did meet him many times, I never learned more about this incident, for he was a man of few words.

Pa's lack of experience in farming, coupled with not being oriented in the natural skills, made for much extra and hard work usually resulting in failure. As we worked, some of the neighbors laughed and called us greenhorns. They ridiculed our city clothes and our combed hair. They described Pa as a beer-belly and said Ma was unfriendly. Although it wasn't said with malice, it hurt a little.

The turnip seed incident may have given our neighbors reason to call us "green." On one of the first days on our place, Pa had gone out to the granary and proceeded to shovel the excessive supply of turnip seeds onto the ground. As the winds blew, the seeds scattered, later to sprout over a wide section.

When one of the Burian boys, out looking for cattle, stopped by, he stared unbelievingly.

"Who in the world dumped those wild turnip seeds out there?" he exclaimed. "Looks like they have took over yer whole field. Ain't goin' to be no wheat grow there. Better get shut o' that pile 'at's left."

Pa was nonplused at the news.

"Wonder if they will burn," he commented as he set a match to the remaining pile.

Woosh! They went up in a sheet of flame to singe his mustache and turn his face to an even redder hue, if indeed that were possible. The fire, aided by the wind, crackled, popped, and spit its way rapidly along the path of stray seeds toward the granary. We had no water to douse the flames and nothing at hand to beat out the fire.

Nick, fortunately, found a shovel by the granary door and hurriedly shoveled away the seeds that lay in the path of the fire. The heat was intense for the moment and then it was over.

Pa sought refuge by venting epithets of derision on Jupe. "That sahlt Johan!" (Salt John is a German term meaning an ignorant person fit only to work in a salt mine.) "Turnip seeds, he says. Turnip seeds! Weed seeds, they are. Now, we grow weeds yet!"

What the Burian boy knew, and we had yet to learn, was that grain is said to be "dirty" when the threshing separator does not do a good job of extracting wild mustard seeds or other weed seeds from flax. In that condition the crop does not bring a good price upon delivery to the grain elevator in town. Cleaning it with a hand operated separator is quite an arduous job.

Pa had seen farming as it was done in "the old country," a boy leading a horse, a man holding the plow. We had to convince him it was best to use one man with four or six horses to a gang plow or harrow. Clinging to the old methods, he started to dig a garden with a hand shovel but soon had to give it up. Nick took over and plowed it up for him one noon when he came in from the field for dinner. Pa insisted it was "a lazy man's way."

While Nick was on an accelerated self-learning program to become a knowledgeable farmer, I hauled the still-frozen manure from dawn to dusk, day after day. My hands became callused, the work more monotonous; I hated it.

As the endless winds swept across the prairie, the days and nights grew warmer. But spring does not come with the first warm breezes. Chill winds and snow flurries still blew across the field where Nick disked, harrowed, and then seeded the wheat. The only happy note was the honking of wedge after wedge of low-flying geese sounding more and more like "Follow me. Follow me." Ducks, too, flew quietly in unpredictable patterns. Sometimes a few would light in the pond, and Pa was more than willing that I take time out for a shoot, for the food I provided.

We were on a panic budget and would continue to be until we had a crop. *If* we had a crop. So much depended on that if. There were the possibilities (yes, even the greater probabilities) of drought, hail, grasshoppers, and the less likely ones of prairie fires, cyclones, grain rust, and insect infestations. Above all, and ever present, was our lack of knowledge about farming.

But spring was arriving, and tiny swords of green pushed their way through layers of old grass. Range animals shed globs of mangy-looking hair revealing shining new coats. We shed our heavy underwear; how good it felt to be light and free!

NEW FRIENDS AND OPPORTUNITIES

SUNDAYS OFFERED our only diversion, for that was the only day of the week we were free from our back-breaking tasks. We could not go far, however, because Pa claimed the horses worked all week and, therefore, we could not have one to use on Sunday. We did not dare point out that it wasn't true—some of the horses didn't do a lick of work all week—nor could we suggest that we too had worked all week.

"You can walk," he told us. It was a seven-mile walk to Vega and back, about an hour and a half each way. We did it once or twice, but it left no room for joy.

Jimmy Havlik, a nephew of store owner Jim Havlik, was my only friend. He rode over on Sundays, and we enjoyed hunting geese, rabbits, and prairie chickens. I even helped him capture a coyote pup he had spent weeks trying to catch. Jim told me the pup would look fully grown by the end of summer, estimating it would weigh about thirty pounds, measure about forty inches including a fifteen-inch tail, and stand about twenty-four inches at the shoulders.

The pup, playful like all young dogs, was the first coyote I had seen up close. The wild dog resembled the wolf but was smaller, with thick fur, grizzled gray above, dark at the shoulders, and buffy underneath. Kutchko, as Jim named him, had the distinguishing pointed muzzle, large pointed ears, long slender legs, and prominent bushy black-tipped tail, drooping low behind the hind legs.

I liked Jim a lot. Fifteen years old, he was one of fifteen brothers and sisters, but only seven were living. Mrs. Havlik's eight other children had died young so she didn't always remember exactly how many there were. Neither she nor anyone else knew the dates the children were born. "Jim," she remembered, "was born in harvest time." None of the children had gone beyond the third grade of school. They had no books nor did they take a newspaper, not even the little four-page Kimball *Graphic* that was printed on one side in the East and finished in Kimball with local ads and gossip. Whatever schooling Jimmy lacked, however, he made up for in his knowledge and skill with horses and guns.

The Havliks were always kind and hospitable as farm people usually are. However, with their large family and small house, Jimmy and I did most of our visiting at our place. The Havlik farmyard was a melange of broken equipment, machinery, harnesses, fences, kitchen utensils, dishes, even dead chickens. The house consisted of a kitchen, one bedroom occupied by Aaron and his wife Stacey, and another room that doubled as a dormitory for the children or as a granary, as the need arose.

From the Havliks I learned there would be quite a few social gatherings to look forward to. Each year after the grain was sold, the farm community customarily enjoyed a series of dances and oyster stew suppers. Refreshments at most of these affairs usually included kolaches, a Bohemian pastry similar to a fruit turnover.

One day, while still at my unhappy task of cleaning the barn, a horseman rode up, followed by a pack of wolfhounds. From previous descriptions by the neighboring farmers, the man could be none other than Sy Singer. He and his hounds were well known, though not favorably. His coyote hunting should have earned the farmers' gratitude, for despite the number killed, coyotes flourished. Their powers of survival seemed to lie in their proverbial wariness and adaptability, and in spite of their well-known curiosity, they were difficult to trap unless a ruse was employed. Coyotes killed game and further annoyed the farmers by killing poultry and occasionally a young calf, goat, or lamb. However in following the predatory prairie wolves, Sy never hesitated to cut barbed wire fences. Even now, his horse and dogs looked tired, and a bloody coyote hide hung from his saddle.

"Hi," he began as he alighted, "I'm Sy Singer. You one of the Beine boys?" As I nodded, he looked pleased. "Good. Is Frank home?" He spoke with an easy familiarity.

No one ever called Pa by his first name. I directed Sy toward the house, saying, "I'll take you up."

He discouraged me, shaking his head. "Better stay here. Keep your eyes on the dogs," he warned. "They would grab one of those chickens in a wink."

Sy looked different from the type of man you would expect in that country. He was cleanshaven and his clothes were of good quality. He wore a sheep-lined jacket, range hat, well-made leather boots, and gloves with red lining. His thin well-groomed mustache added to his charming demeanor. I judged him to be in his early thirties. His horse, eating from a pile of hay, appeared to be a good one. Opposite the coyote hide, a rifle and scabbard hung from the saddle. The hounds, panting while trying to watch both me and the chickens, bore numerous scars along with more recent wounds inflicted by coyotes.

Shadows were lengthening by the time Sy and Pa emerged from the house, arm in arm. Both were in a gay mood, with Sy laughing boisterously and Pa making an attempt at dignity, face flushed, trying to keep his balance. As he dropped his freshly lighted cigar, Sy retrieved it for him.

I could tell Pa had something on his mind. "George, Sy wants you to work for him," he said in a tone of approval.

"Yes," added Sy. "I want someone to help Fanny, my wife. She runs the place while I buy and sell horses."

Any change, any new experience, would have been acceptable to me. I had been working on our farm about a month, and I was tired of hauling manure. Pa was disagreeable much of the time; he found fault because he didn't know how to do things himself. Moreover, I could easily be spared. Since we had farm equipment for only one man, the farming was Nick's task. All of the other work I had been doing around the place could probably be finished by Eddie. The country school-year is short and he would soon have full days at home. Agnes, too, would then be home all day, and she seemed to enjoy helping Ma with almost everything inside the house. I indicated I was pleased with Pa's decision.

After Sy left, however, Pa and Ma must have had a hassle.

"There is work to be done around here," I heard Ma say. "That Singer, I don't trust him. He doesn't look like a farmer to me. Sending that boy out to work—what are you thinking of?"

It must be hard, I reasoned, for a mother to see a son or daughter leave home for the first time. Pa didn't say anything, which was sort of unusual for him.

Before noon Sunday, two of the Runge boys, Tater and Goos, came over. It was their first visit.

"Not Tater," he corrected. "It's Tador, and it ain't Goos, either. It's Gus. Short for Theodore and August." Their mixture of German and English was hard to understand.

"Gonna work for Singer, ya?" questioned Tater or Tador. "How's he gonna pay ya? He ain't got nothin', a real nothin'," he emphasized. "Gets some boot on a horse trade, bounty on coyotes, traps a little, spends it on booze."

"Ya," put in Gus, "Boozin', cuttin' fences, rustlin', tain't nothin' to *claim jumpin'*."

Their story was somewhat difficult to follow, but I gathered that a fellow whose Indian wife had died got a job at the Saunders ranch quite a number of years ago, and brought his only child, a little girl, with him. Shortly thereafter, he left for Mobridge in the northern part of the state to get work on either the Standing Rock or Cheyenne River where the government was supplying the Indians with large herds of cattle. He was to come back to get his half-breed daughter, Fanny.

Something dire surely must have happened, for he never returned. In fact, he was not even heard from afterwards, perhaps because he could neither read nor write. The Saunders continued to care for Fanny as they did for their own child. They sent her to school, but she was unhappy there, neither playing with other children nor giving attention to her studies. Instead, taking her school lunch with her, she would guide her old horse out somewhere on the prairie where she would stay until dark. Later on Mr. Saunders gave her a good horse and a dog, and she spent the days looking after cattle. Because of her refusal to associate with people, some thought she was odd.

A few years later part of the Crow Reservation where Fanny helped tend the Saunders's herds was thrown open for settlement. Fanny knew every inch of that country. With the help of Mr. Saunders, who by now she called her Paw, she filed on a choice half section. It was, in fact, the only claim on which there was a bubbling spring and a small lake.

With a little help she built a cabin on a knoll that overlooked a lush little valley and from where she could see scrub oaks and wild plums growing along the banks of Crow Creek. Fanny seemed to like living alone. She had a vegetable garden, chickens, a cow or two, her horse, and a dog. She fenced the barnyard, using Indian poles and two-strand barbed wire. Around the spring and little lake she used sturdy pine posts bought at the lumber yard and six strands of cattle-proof wire. She thought she had everything to be desired.

Before one could get a title of ownership, or a "patent" as it was called, the settler had to "prove up," that is, furnish proof that all conditions of the Homestead Act had been met. One condition required that a habitable dwelling be built. It could be of sod, wood, or some of each, or it could even be a dugout, but it had to be occupied a specified number of months each year for five years.

In order to file, one had to be of legal age and have taken out his first papers indicating the intention of becoming a citizen of the United States. Many homesteaders failed to stay and relinquished their claims. Their land was given back to the government to be filed on again by someone who, as it was said, "bet the government that he could stick it out for the five years before starving to death." "Relinquishments" were usually land that was almost worthless to begin with.

Anyone so low and mean as to report someone who was not meeting the conditions of the law, or who determined that the claim holder was under legal age at the time of filing, could be rewarded with permission to take the claim. Such property became known as a pre-emption. Pre-emptors sought out the very best pieces of land to steal legally, but they were held in contempt by others.

It was by this process that Fanny lost all her claim rights to a stranger by the name of Patrick "Sy" Singer. It wasn't known what the grounds were, but most likely she had misstated her age. There were some hard feelings in the community, but they were assuaged when it became known that Sy and Fanny had married.

The women who met Sy were envious. "She is a lucky girl," most of them agreed. "She not only gets to keep her land but gets a man to work it. He's handsome, polished, educated, a snazzy dresser, and—gosh, can he dance!"

Tador disagreed. "He gets the land, he gets a cook, and she does the work."

"Anyway, he did the right thing by her," Gus drawled.

"Right thin', my eye, betcha any money he proves up, he sells out, and gives her the heave-ho—a dirty claim jumper, that's all he is!"

I was glad Ma hadn't invited them in. Had she heard any of this, my job would be out of the question. As far as I was concerned, what they had said made no difference. I wanted to get away from home and everything had been decided. I was to leave Sunday afternoon and would go to work on Monday.

S Y ' S

❖

MY ARRIVAL

S Y SINGER's homestead was considered close enough to our place for me to walk. Since I would be coming home each weekend, leaving Saturday night and returning Sunday afternoon, I needed to take only my work clothes and toilet articles. With these belongings I headed due west following the directions Sy had given me. As I crossed one more rise in the prairie, their place came into view.

The cabin Sy and Fanny lived in was small, unpainted, and set up on field stones. Two other structures were built of Indian poles, flat on top, and covered with dry grass or hay.

A few yards from the cabin, the fierce barking and leaping of Sy's dogs caused me to stop still, shielding myself with the flour sack containing my few possessions. At once, Fanny came to the door and dispersed them with some blue-blazing, well-chosen words. "Some vocabulary," I gulped, inaudibly.

Without greeting or introduction, the short slightly-built woman said, "Quite a walk. Come in. I'll make some tea." Fanny was not one to waste words on conversation or civilities. There was no mistaking her being part Indian; she had a round face, long black braids, and half-squinted eyes. Her attire did nothing to enhance her looks, although with a little effort she could have been quite attractive. She was wearing a slate gray shapeless dress and boys' shoes.

As Fanny fed cow chips into a tiny stove, I looked about the room. It was sparsely furnished with a kitchen table, one bench, two chairs, and a cupboard made of wooden boxes. The stove had been set up on bricks to add height. Next to it was a fuel box filled with chips. This one room served as kitchen, living room, and dining room. The windows, one at each end, were without curtains. A rifle and a shotgun hung on nails over a doorway that led to a lean-to. Every cabin I had seen so far in this country had one or more lean-tos. On another nail, to the right side of the doorway, hung a banjo and a large sack of Corn Cake smoking tobacco. Both interested me. I wouldn't mind trying the tobacco, and who, I wondered, played the banjo. I decided it wasn't Sy and that it had to be Fanny. Perhaps we would have some music? What songs would she sing? Indian ones, I hoped.

In the lean-to where I put my flour sack there was scarcely room for a double bed and a cot. The bed, which I correctly took to be Fanny and Sy's, could be hidden from my view by drawing together some bright calico curtains that hung from binder twine. My cot, against the wall sideways, allowed wall space for hangers where I hung my work clothes.

Judging from the surroundings, the meager furnishings, and particularly the tiny stove, I hardly expected such a good meal as we had that evening. I thought it might be a special "first night dinner," but it proved to be typical of meals that followed. My stay at Sy's was my first experience of consistently having all I could eat. Fanny set bountiful tables with wild or domestic fried chicken and excellent vegetables from her garden. I remember best the potatoes and real cream gravy, the freshly baked hot pies, and bowls of wild plums with rich cream. At our house, Ma always divided one roast chicken among six of us. Here Fanny fried two chickens for the three of us, and Sy customarily ate little since his forte was fresh biscuits and chicken gravy.

Throughout the first several weeks, my days were spent in the field. Black ribbons of sod turned over the moldboard of my plow, one mile each round, thirty rounds a day. My eyes focused constantly on a spot slightly ahead, on the lookout for rocks. There weren't many, but only one unnoticed rock poking through the sod could mean disaster. The plow thrown out could crack my ribs, or if the point of it were to catch under a boulder there would be a sudden dead stop, and something would have to give. Fortunately my eyesight was good and I was alert, and no such accident occurred.

Sea gulls followed me in my work, picking grubs that wriggled in the fresh soil. They were beautiful birds, slightly smaller and less noisy than those in ocean areas. Known as herring gulls, they came from Lake Superior and some of the smaller lakes of Minnesota. I wondered where the birds went at night—into trees? . . . tall grass? . . . low bushes? . . . sheltered logs?

Prairie dogs popped out of their burrows in futile attempts to frighten me away with their barking. A prairie chicken would often stay under cover until the horses' feet were almost upon it. A gopher snake, gorged with food and scarcely able to move, would lie inert, to be plowed under. A meadow lark could alert me to its nest by its wild gyrations, and I would plow around it. Throughout each day the ever-present wind continued, sometimes fierce, but mostly gentle.

Fanny had a sister Mary, better known as "Sis." They were, of course, not real sisters; Sis was the Saunders's daughter. She was lithe and willowy, prettier than most girls, with soft light brown hair. Her face and arms were that flattering shade a tan becomes after fading through the winter. She smelled of fresh soap, and her clothes always seemed clean and new, whether she was wearing boots-and-buckskin or ribbons-and-lace.

I remember the impression she made on me that first Sunday afternoon she rode up. I had never noticed girls much in Omaha, but I noticed her! Perhaps it was the way she was dressed, or the way she sat her horse. Or perhaps it was the horse itself! Dismounting, she tossed the reins to me.

"Here, boy, loosen her cinch. Not too much water. A gallon of oats." It was more like a command than a request.

As she turned toward the cabin, I took hold of the pommel and prepared to place my foot in a stirrup.

"Don't you dare!" she shrieked. "No one rides Molly. No one has ever been on Molly, ever! Do you want to spoil her?"

From that moment I hated her. I should perhaps have been thankful I didn't get onto Molly after all, since she pranced and sun-fished when Sis left, but I wasn't.

Sis's visits on the following Sundays were even worse. I was disgusted with the way she fawned over Sy, trimming his nails. Whereas Fanny's hands were hard and callused, his were lily white, always protected by gloves. Sis rubbed pomade into his hair, laughed at his jokes, and sang to the accompaniment of his banjo. To my surprise, I had discovered it was Sy, not Fanny, who played the banjo.

Fanny didn't seem to notice Sis's special attentions to Sy. One day when she complained about Sy's failure to help with the farm work I sensed the opportunity I had been waiting for. I asked her if Sis's seemingly unwarranted attention to Sy didn't bother her. Fanny replied, "No. What she does for him, I don't have to do."

I didn't dislike Sy; after all, he wasn't the one who was making the play. In fact, when Sis wasn't around, he was a great guy to me. I was doing a man's work and liked to be treated as a man; it was a new experience for me. Sy and I shared our tobacco. I never bought any liquor, but Sy urged his on me whenever he had it—usually straight alcohol in black coffee. I returned around noon on Sundays from my weekend trips home and Sy and I always hunted together on those afternoons before Sis got there. He would tell me of things only an older man would know about.

Sy said someday he was going to quit clod hoppin', sell the homestead, and get himself a bar or poolroom in Cleveland, where he had come from. Fanny was not included in his plans. In fact, he never spoke of her except to say in a deprecating way, "An Indian is always an Indian." He said she had some funny ideas and believed in queer things about that spring and little lake, for example.

"Don't go near there," he warned. "She would kill you. She has it fenced up hog tight. Some stupid idea; I don't get the drift."

One thing bothered me, however. Sy knew I didn't like Sis's treating me as though I were just any old hired hand. I felt he could have done something to build me up in some way for there were opportunities. I could have liked Sis, and Sy realized that I longed for a little attention from her. She was so pretty, and her tinkling laughter really got to me.

MANLY ADVENTURES

I HAD YET to really learn about my employer. I thought little about Gus and Tador's words about Sy as the weeks wore on, and I accepted him at face value. I particularly enjoyed our hunting expeditions, glad to be accepted, and proud that he thought me equal to participate.

One Sunday when Sy and I started out, he said we'd go hunting over on the reservation. It didn't occur to me at the time to wonder if this was legal or if we would be trespassing. After all, I was the newcomer and would not have questioned our right to invade the Crow lands in search of game any more than I would have challenged any other site Sy selected.

Upon reaching the reservation, we hitched our horses to the fence, took our guns, and walked in. Our entry seemed surprisingly easy (but why did I think so unless I felt somehow we had no business being there). As we proceeded along a draw, shooting a prairie chicken here and there, we were suddenly startled by a herd of cattle headed toward us. We did not know where they had come from and did not have time to wonder. They had no doubt become disturbed by the report of our guns.

At Sy's suggestion, "We better get out of here," we took off on a fast walk.

With the cattle coming faster, we increased our pace to a trot and finally ran as fast as we could. Faster and still faster the cattle came, gaining on us. There seemed to be hundreds, with hoofs beating the ground in a louder and louder roar. Their white faces and red rumps undulated in waves as, with tails flying, they rent the air with bawling.

Their pounding hoofs raised huge clouds of dust. We could feel the tremor of the earth close behind us. We thought we were helpless. Just ahead was a culvert, and there was a slim chance we might reach it. The culvert was only a few old planks, very low, over a wash. Would the opening be large enough to crawl into? It was, but just barely. Sy crawled into one side and I the other. We huddled there in a bed of spiny Russian thistle that was moldy and damp.

Cattle milled around us. A large bull tore up turf and bellowed. With one twist of his huge horns, he could have pulled up the weathered planks.

When we were able to get our breath, Sy spoke. "They may have stopped. But then again, one might charge—a mean bull or a cow with a lost or bawling calf."

We had to stay hunched up in the cramped quarters for a long time, thistles no longer affording protection from the dirty water under us. Snakes slithered around, and the cattle moved about outside, grazing. It looked like a long wait.

"Maybe we could stampede them." We agreed on a plan. With Sy on one side and me on the other, we would rush out together shooting off our guns, shouting and waving our arms.

"Now!" Sy gave the signal.

Out I jumped, according to plan, shooting my single barrel. The startled cattle faced me, hesitating. Would they charge? I took a few steps forward, shooting lower over them. My number six shot sprayed those farther away; they turned, kicked up their heels, raised their tails, and ran. Others followed. One bull held his ground for a moment; another shot and he too turned.

Then Sy came out to help, after the entire herd was already in full stampede. I wondered why Sy had not come out at the time he gave the signal. As we left, I noticed how mussed his clothes were, in contrast to his usual impeccable appearance. He had also lost his birds; for some reason I still had mine. When we arrived home, Sis was there.

"We were caught in a stampede," Sy explained while we shaved and changed clothes. He told Sis in detail how he had maneuvered the situation to our advantage, permitting our escape.

"Dear, dear! Goodness me! You could have been killed," exclaimed Sis, laying her hand on his arm.

Fanny was busy at the stove. It appeared she wasn't even listening.

Sy, the big hero! I wished I could tell Sis my version, the way it really happened. I could also have told her about the time a few weeks before when Sy and I went over to Fort Thompson for a few head of steers. The day was nice enough when we started out, with no indication of rain; but we had barely begun our return trip when a terrific storm broke.

When gumbo soil is thoroughly wet it is sticky, but when it

is wet only on top it acts like grease with hard ground underneath. Our horses and the cattle slithered and slid. When the cattle finally refused to face the driving wind and rain, we were forced to abandon them.

Even then, minus the cattle, we couldn't make time. We were still a considerable distance from home, and it was already dark. The rain came down in torrents. Lightning flashed around us as claps of thunder indicated its close range. We knew there could be a number of direct hits. Having given no thought to taking rain gear, we were soaked to the skin.

Blinded as we were by alternate blackness and illuminating flashes, we scarcely knew we had arrived home until we realized our plodding horses had come to a halt. Sy dismounted and rushed for the house. I thought I heard his voice between claps of thunder. He must have shouted, "Put the horses in the barn."

It took a while to unsaddle, feed, and dry the horses. I also had difficulty with the barbed wire corral gate, which was never in repair. By the time I got into the house, Sy was nowhere in sight. I looked around, questioningly.

"He's in bed," Fanny said.

His clothes were hanging on a stretch of binder twine, dripping into a wash tub.

"What about supper?" I inquired.

"He won't eat any supper—not now anyway with this lightning. He may get up later. Put on some dry clothes, and we'll go ahead with ours."

When we had our dinner at noon the next day Sy was not around. Fanny felt there was a need to say something in his defense.

"There's a lot of folks won't touch a wire when it's lightning. You see bones in the corner of some pastures; them are what's left when cattle gets struck. Wet hide touches the wire on one side— another critter is against the other wire. Lightning kills them and all those in between, six or eight at a time."

"There *is* a bunch of bones in one corner of our pasture," I said, realizing the full import of her words and remembering my struggle with the wire corral gate last night.

"Yeh, them were horses," Fanny nodded. "Henzlik's horses— happened about five years ago, when I first moved up here. There will be more get killed. There always is."

FANNY SEEMED quite content with her isolated life and apparently had never had an urgent need for either contact or conversation with many people. She didn't talk much; but, of course, she couldn't have had much to talk about, never having been more than a few miles from home. Not knowing how to read or write, she never got a letter or a newspaper or any kind of mail. She kept to herself and had no social contacts; no visitors other than Sis. The only thing she ever talked about, outside of work, was the little lake. She became animated and even smiled when talking about that special place. She always spoke as though everything had taken place a long time ago and as if she had been reincarnated, although of course she wouldn't have known anything about that.

I wondered if Fanny knew the meaning of loneliness; she had evidently been alone by choice most of her life. As a young girl with her horse and dog looking after the Saunders cattle she was far happier than during any hour spent in the schoolhouse. Except for seeing that her herds did not stray, Fanny spent most of her childhood with the birds and little animals that lived at, or came to, the lake.

Whenever Fanny reminisced about the little lake, she never referred to herself as "I," but always as "the little girl." She said "the little girl" shared her bread with the small animals and that they ate from her hand: mallards, with shiny green heads and orange bills; smaller ducks such as teals with green or blue on their wings; tiny rabbits she could hold in her hands; and other kinds of birds including snipes, some with long bills and spindly legs. Her favorites were the black birds with red wings and golden eyes. Although she didn't know the names of most, she described all of them so vividly from her keen observations that I knew exactly which ones she had seen.

The red-winged blackbirds built their nests, bowl shaped and rather bulky, of grasses and weed stalks suspended from cattails drawn together. The tall marsh plants with their long flat leaves carefully concealed the nests. She would watch the birds work for days until the nest was lined with finer grass and rootlets. One morning to her delight an egg would appear and then others appeared until usually there were four. When the young were hatched the mother fed them with some of "the little girl's" bread.

On top of the fallen rushes in the marsh, ducks built their nests of reeds and grasses, warmly lined them with breast feathers and down, and laid their eggs. When "the little girl" took a freshly laid one to eat, another would appear in its place.

Fanny described in detail her life at the little lake. She watched for spring arrivals and fall migrations of birds, noticed wilting flowers and falling leaves, felt touches of frost and tested coatings of ice, examined leaf buds and tiny blossoms, waited for thick dense growth to shelter little creatures, and marveled at these mysteries of nature unfolding before her. She was, as she said, "never alone."

"Birds and animals don't talk—yet they understand. You don't have to talk."

The lake had belonged to the Indians. Wa Sau (Grease) was angry with her for having fenced the lake. For many moons before white men came, longer than any old man of the tribe remembered, the lake had been part of the marriage ritual. The young brave and his intended bride went to the waters; upon their return the marriage feast was celebrated. They were man and wife. As she told the story, a faraway look engulfed Fanny's eyes and features, for she was building dreams.

"Some day I will build my house there," she would always say as she finished talking about the lake. "No one goes there now—'the little girl' doesn't go there—no one goes there any more. You must not go there." The admonition seemed neither a threat nor warning; she wasn't looking at me when she said it. Yet, the intended meaning was clear.

Spring turned to summer. The flax field blossomed into a carpet of blue so dense it looked as though it could be walked upon. Corn leaves rustled in the wind, reaching across the rows to touch each other, and nubbins of tassels began to peep through. Wheat, chest high, was beginning to ripen into golden grain.

Newcomers, including Pa, began to speak confidently of harvest time while those experienced settlers warily watched the sky and said nothing. They knew all too well the disaster a mere couple weeks of scorching wind with no rain could bring, the havoc a cloud of locusts could do in only two days, and how a hailstorm could in less than an hour transform a green field of grain into brown rubble so chewed and pounded into the earth it might as well never have existed. All these thoughts were too horrible to dwell upon. I felt good and did not want anything to mar my pleasure.

My chief concern for the moment was that little lake. I wanted to see it. Why shouldn't I? There was no good reason. It was just a clear case of oversentimentality on Fanny's part. I could understand, though, that to one like Fanny who had so little, small things loom large.

On hot, humid summer days in South Dakota the temperature may occasionally rise into the 90s, or even well over 100. Then, if ever, a bath is a luxury. On this day, sweaty and dirty, I even would have welcomed an opportunity to cool only my tired, burning feet. I headed for the lake.

From the high side, I saw the little lake as it widened out and away. In the open places among the cattails were a few ducks and a number of red-winged blackbirds. As I approached, I looked down into a sort of grotto. Water was running along moss-covered ledges, over lichen-etched rocks, to drip and blip into the crystal pool. Protected by the continuous shade of overhanging rim rocks, it looked cool and inviting.

It was a typical summer day, with the air scented by the blossoms of wild plum, chokecherry, and buffalo berry. I resisted a cooling splash only because of my aversion to putting on my dirty sweaty clothes afterwards. Tomorrow, I promised myself, I would return.

The following day, as I drew near with a change of clothing under my arm, I was astonished at the sight of Molly grazing nearby. At almost the same instant, she raised her head, straightened her ears, and was apparently about to nicker when she recognized me and resumed her grazing. My first thought was that she had strayed, but closer inspection showed she had been picketed. I had a moment of indecision, but curiosity prevailed. I moved cautiously, listening. Fanny had said, "No one goes there."

There wasn't a sound except a light rustling of leaves as a friendly breeze blew toward me. My caution went with it as I crawled on my stomach, out of view, behind a large rock and peeked over. A feeling of guilt crept over me when I saw her

clothes piled neatly, and then, her beside them. Sis lay with her
head on her arm, face down. Her long, light brown hair covered
her face, arms, and shoulders. Leafy shadows danced on her
slender body.

Indignation welled within me, and I moved away. How dare
Sis disregard Fanny and sneak to the lake! Whatever pleasure the
sight of Sis might have given me was nullified by her betrayal of
Fanny's trust that "no one goes there."

LEGGETT'S PARIS GREEN OR DRY
POWDER GUN.
For Orchard, Vineyard,
Garden or Potato Field.
Distributes Paris Green,
Sulphur, "Fungiroid," (a
powdered Bordeaux Mix-
ture) or any dry powder.
THOUSANDS IN USE
Illustrated Circular on
application.

A
Won-
derful
Inven-
tion
Light,
Swift,
Easy,
Safe,
Strong
and
Cheap.

PROGRESS AT THE HOME PLACE

I HAD GONE to Sy's with the understanding that I would go
home every weekend, but it soon became obvious weekly
trips were out of the question. Sy offered no encouragement in the way of a horse to ride, so I was compelled to make the
long walk after dark on Saturday night. I was pretty tired after
putting in a full day of work, and walking after dark was more
difficult than striding along in daylight. To have me stay over,
Sy used other means besides tacitly refusing me the use of a horse.
He would casually mention that snakes come out during the cool
of the night and would caution me not to step on a rattler.

Several weeks away from home at a time, however, was
enough. I had no desire to break the home ties and, besides, Sy
was always able to find something other than the usual chores
to be done on Sunday. Braving the dark and the unknown, I
would periodically set out for home.

What did Fanny mean, I wondered, when she said, "Sy
wouldn't go afoot at night"? Was he too much of a coward? Or
was he just using good sense?

As it turned out I saw no snakes, but I was occasionally

startled when an equally frightened steer or horse would jump up just ahead.

On my visits home, I could see all was not going well on the farm. The general atmosphere was far from serene. With the first heavy rain our dam, built without proper ballast, went out. Not only did all of our work go for naught, but also we earned the ire of the Burians when the unusual rush of water down the draw strained their dam beyond capacity and it too went out. For this they never did forgive us.

Food storage was another problem we had not mastered. A few people built icehouses or caves into side slopes covered with earth and sod. They enjoyed ice until late fall. Our ice melted shortly after it was stored, our meat spoiled, and butter turned to rancid oil.

The garden Pa started was far from flourishing. When the young potato plants came up, they became infested with potato bugs and upset the tranquility of the family. Pa had the whole family out picking potato bugs; they picked pails of them. The more they picked, the more the bugs came. One Sunday when I was home, he ordered me to join in. I refused and told him the job could be accomplished best with a spray of Paris green which everyone else used. Crawling and stooping in the heat of the day picking those green, spitting, soft bugs is just about the most disagreeable job imaginable, especially when there is an easier way. But Pa would have none of "that spray method" until finally forced to it by the lack of cooperation from the family. They could no longer keep ahead of the bugs, and the plants were almost stripped of leaves.

Information I was bringing home of better and easier ways to perform various farm tasks was rarely acceptable to Pa, but Nick was eager to profit by it. Fortunately, as time went on, Pa turned more and more of the farm management over to Nick.

Pa was clearly out of his environment and having difficulty adjusting, so was consequently irritable. He knew nothing about farming, and city life had made him soft. His pattern in Omaha had been to rise late, spend a few hours visiting with customers, then take a few orders after cigars and a beer. He had always been fastidious in his attire, wearing a clean pink pin-stripe cotton flannel shirt each day. Ma had to make them herself since his large size was not available in stores. Frequent washing on a hand washboard took an early toll, causing Ma to make these shirts, as well as our flannel nightshirts, by the dozen. Now, on the farm,

Pa was wearing the slightly worn shirts, his black homburg hats, soft congress gaiter shoes, and other city-type clothes. These habits of dress, along with his smoking cigars and drinking bottled beer on weekdays, branded him as different. He was aloof with neighbors, never visiting or taking part in any of their interests. Their comments made me uncomfortable. But when I quoted from something I had read, "When in Rome, do as the Romans," I incurred Pa's ire.

"Why should I live like these honyockers?" he raged.

Nick was the only one who really got along with Pa, and that was only because he ignored him, though not with any real intent. It was Nick's nature to be quiet and easy going, and he was never more content than when out in the fields alone. Taking time out only to eat and sleep, he was responsible for whatever success occurred. Without him the farm most likely would have been a total failure.

AN OLD INTEREST REVIVED

As SUMMER PROGRESSED I was going home more often. With the later sunsets, I did not mind the walk home since most of it could be covered during twilight. During these twilight walks home, I listened to the coyotes as they sang in chorus. One would start with a series of short barks which gradually increased in rapidity and volume until they merged into a long yell. Others joined in and the chorus continued for a minute or two, then was repeated with intermittent pauses. Two or three coyotes frequently sang together, and the songs of several groups would ring over the prairie.

Cool evening breezes also helped make the hikes more pleasant. It was not like the miserable heat I remembered in Omaha when Ma, insisting on keeping city windows closed, would dampen our sheets in the night to cool us.

By mid-summer I was going home every weekend for Sunday baseball games, which we had enjoyed sandlot style in Omaha. On my Sundays home we had given up hunting, for which I had more zeal, to playing ball, at which Nick excelled. We never hunted together much after the Sunday two prairie chickens flew up ahead of us. I shot at and dropped the one nearer my side, at the same time yelling, "Shoot!" and indicating the one on his side.

"Oh, it's too far," he drawled.

During that brief interval, I had reloaded my single barrel but found the bird was then out of range. In frustration and anger, I raised my gun and threw a parting shot. To my utter amazement, the chicken stopped in flight, changed course, flew straight up, and fell to the ground with a thud. While picking it later, I found not a trace of a shot or even a break in the skin, only a small red dot at the base of the head.

Baseball for us had moved from the farmyard to a real diamond. Nick was getting ten dollars each Sunday to pitch for the Kimball team. I joined the team because he thought he could be more effective if I would do the catching. Like the rest of the team members, I got no pay other than expenses. Playing ball was fun for us, and we soon learned hometowners were eager to back their teams with money. We took all the bets we could get, but it was too good to last. As Nick's pitching reputation became known, there were no more betting offers, except from us. Even with our most liberal odds there were no takers.

As the Kimball team enjoyed more and more scoreboard success, we began to have difficulty getting opponents. Nick could predict with uncanny certainty the number of runs he would allow. I begged him to take it easy and he would, for awhile, but he loved baseball and played mainly for the joy of it. He often let the other team get ahead, and then bore down with a low fastball.

His saying "You get on base, and I'll drive you in" made for an almost automatic run.

Games in various other towns were the same as attending a picnic. Particularly enjoyable were the games with the Indians. With much free time spent in practice, they had an excellent team of near professional quality. If they had only been able to stay away from whiskey and allow themselves to be managed! One never was quite sure a game with them would go the full nine innings.

I thought it a tragedy that Nick should want to waste his life as a dirt farmer after he received an offer to go into professional baseball. There were so many advantages to baseball life: the excitement of the crowds, riding on a Pullman train to many cities and towns, staying at nice hotels, being served a variety of delectable foods, and having long vacations that could be spent hunting and fishing. Even at this time Nick's services were in such demand that whenever we were without transportation we were furnished with an Overland automobile and chauffeur who would come out to get us. It was probably the only automobile in Kimball.

In later years old timers in the area would say, "The Beine boys—yes, I remember them. They were good ball players." This included our brother Ed, who joined the team and played with enthusiasm and skill. A few years later, he attended St. Mary's College in Oakland, California (the campus has since moved to Moraga), on a baseball scholarship.

While our baseball activities were increasing, another change was occurring with my employer. Sy was coming home less often, and there were reports of his drinking and fighting. Anyone who loved peace had to give him a wide berth.

One night I was awakened from a sound sleep by shouts and curses outside the cabin. At first I thought Sy's threats and accusations were directed to someone out in the yard with him. As I distinguished a few words, there was no doubt as to whom he meant.

"That . . . half-breed! I'll kill her, and him, too!" Sy shouted. "I'll cut his throat! He's in there with my wife!" Two pistol shots followed in rapid succession.

I was terrified. I knew that a fellow in such a drunken rage might do anything. As he continued to threaten us, I hurriedly but quietly took the .25-20 off the nails. Back in my bed I pointed the gun toward the door, my finger ready on the trigger.

"Stop right there!" I rehearsed the words under my breath. Poor Fanny, I thought. She must be in a state of shock, from fear.

There had been no sound from Fanny's side of the curtain, but now she spoke in her usual slow monotone: "You won't need that. That bastard knows better than to come in here."

I didn't know what she meant, but soon all was quiet. Sy wasn't around the following morning, and Fanny made no mention of the incident, for it may have been "only an incident" to her. To me it was a terrifying nightmare that left a knot in the pit of my stomach.

I had begun to wonder about my wages. Sy was now two

month behind in paying me for my work, and Pa was insisting on my getting the money because he and the family needed it. I kept remembering that Gus and Tador had been dubious about the pay, the whole arrangement for that matter. I told Fanny I would have to find another job.

After that frightening experience, she didn't blame me for wanting to quit.

"Sy should be doing the work anyway," she commented. "Go to work for Paw," she suggested. "Thirty dollars a month, year 'round."

That was top pay, and I was pleased with Fanny's suggestion that I work at the Saunders place.

SAUNDERS'S RANCH

❖

A SAUNDERS MAN

THE NEXT WEEKEND at home I was able to tell the folks Fanny had talked to Mr. Saunders and reported that "Paw," as she called him, was agreeable to hiring me. She had made all the arrangements. I was to leave the following Sunday for my new job.

Nick had agreed the team could get along without me that Sunday, since the end of the baseball season was near, "in fact, for the few remaining games, if necessary." I knew it was important to arrive for a new job rested. The excitement and strain of meeting new people, learning a new routine, and adjusting to my new life on the Saunders ranch would be enough to wear me out.

Naturally, Ma was pleased. "I never did think Sy a fit person for a young boy to be around. He couldn't be a good influence. I'm glad George is getting away from there," she told Pa. "What about his pay? Will he receive his wages?"

Pa said he would have a talk with Sy.

All that week, though I was busy and worked hard, the time dragged. At last, Sunday arrived. Sis came sometime around noon for one of her usual visits and, at the same time, to get me. She looked so small behind her father's lively black team hitched to the top buggy with the yellow wheels.

Sy, who was angry, was nowhere to be seen. After a brief visit with Fanny, we were off on a fast trot. Sis was all business. When I thanked her for coming to get me, she brushed the favor off quickly: "I was coming over anyhow. Driving the buggy to pick you up was at Father's request."

I was a bit embarrassed by her queenly superiority, so I could think of little to talk about. I did say that my stay at Sy's had been, for the most part, quite pleasant. Perhaps I was not so discreet as I should have been when I then blurted out something about her attentions to Sy, because she immediately showed her displeasure.

"That is a facetious thing to say, and you should know better. Being nice to Sy is only for Fanny's sake. She has an unfortunate background and has little to offer a man like Sy."

My thoughts were drawn to Sis and all she had to offer. I was alone with her now as I had often longed to be, in a beautiful setting on a gorgeous summer day, and—nothing! She broke up an awkward silence with "Look at that tiny colt; it can't be more than a day or two old." I had already seen it make awkward little jumps on weak, spindly legs in an attempt to keep up with its mother as she continued to graze.

It was good to see Sis smile at the little flickertails bobbing in jerks from their burrows to watch us with unblinking, marble-like eyes. As she watched them I, in turn, feasted my eyes upon her.

When we reached Gannvalley, which was about halfway in our eleven-mile journey, she stopped in front of a flimsy-looking frame building. "I'll be a few minutes," she announced. "I want to pick up our mail."

While waiting I noted the road, gouged and furrowed during the wet spring, and now turned to dust. A few saddlehorses and a team hitched to a farm wagon dozed at a hitching bar while flies continuously rose and settled on mounds of dung. The few squat ugly buildings with their false fronts looked cheerless and gray. From the laughter that came through the open double doorway, it was apparent Sis was enjoying a visit with a man in the combination store-post office. This delay gave me a moment to look through a book of English poems I had found behind the seat of the buggy.

When Sis reappeared, she was in good spirits from having received a letter. From her comments I assumed it to be from someone quite similar to the buttermaker in Vega I had heard about. She referred to him as the "creamery man" and said he was a lot of fun and a college man which, indeed, was a distinction in itself.

"Speaking of school," I said, "I'm glad to know that you enjoy poetry. My favorite is *Thanatopsis*," which indeed it was, because having been forced to learn it in school it was the only one I knew. After reciting several stanzas, I went into mental handsprings with a line from this stanza and a line from that, hoping to lead her to believe I knew the entire poem. She seemed impressed beyond my expectations, which encouraged me to quote some humorous lines less strange to me.

"This one," I said, "was written by Eugene Field for the benefit of a neighbor girl, when he was about eleven years old:

> Oh had I wings of a dove I would fly
> Away from this world of fleas
> I'd fly around Miss Emerson's yard
> And light on Miss Emerson's trees.

Whether Eugene Field wrote this or not made little difference. Sis placed a hand on my arm and seemed to sit a little closer. With my repertoire about exhausted, I was pleased when she changed the subject by sharing some chewy candy with me. It smelled of Djer Kiss perfume, as did almost everything about her.

After that we had many things to talk about. We were just dawdling along, seemingly reluctant to reach our destination, when "Golly, gee whiz!" she exclaimed, slapping the reins lightly, "We better get going. We've been on the road for two hours!"

The Saunders ranch, extending along the Crow Creek bottom, came into full view as we began to descend a long slope. I could see the corrals and the big red barn, with its wide doors and cupola, surrounded by smaller buildings. The two-story white house with a low picket fence and a flower garden looked friendly and inviting. A whirling windmill added life and movement to the picture. The creek beyond widened in places to form large pools, its course traced by low-growing trees along its banks. The Saunders ranch was indeed a contrast to Sy and Fanny's place.

Mr. Saunders, slightly hunched over, was considerably older than his attractive wife. Both were English and had come to the United States by way of Canada. Mr. Saunders took me to the barn, where he introduced me to Al, who was unharnessing the team. Al, about my age, became my bunk mate, reluctantly at first, as he felt somewhat superior around cattle and horses. He had a rowdy, hard look to him, intensified by a slightly drooping eyelid and a broken tooth. His way of standing on the edge of his cowboy boots with a thumb hooked in his belt and a badly rolled cigarette drooping from one side of his mouth made him seem even tougher.

I got settled in the bunkhouse just before time for supper. We had Jello for dessert. I had never tasted it before and found that I liked it. It was cool and had a pretty translucent red color and a nice fruitlike flavor.

My job would include care of the horses except the two cared for by Bert, the stud horse man who worked for Mr. Saunders for only one season each year. Bert was seldom at the ranch since his duties took him to various small towns where, as his handbills and posters announced, the stallion would be "AT STUD." I was pleased I would be looking after Mr. Saunders's beautiful blacks which he drove around the country buying cattle, and Sis's Molly, when she wasn't taking care of her horse herself.

After helping with the chores, I went to bed anticipating pleasant days.

MY BUNK MATE AND THE DUKE

DURING OUR OFF HOURS Al and I had little contact with the other men on the ranch, except on some Saturday evenings when he took up a small collection which totaled a dollar, the price of a full quart of Old Crow. Everyone drank from the bottle and there was no way to measure, but from all appearances I was sure Al drank at least two shares. In high spirits he would entertain us with off-key dirty parodies of "The Old Chisholm Trail," some of which, no doubt, he made up himself.

Al, a fast and tireless worker, was awake at daybreak each morning, into his jeans and boots after having a cigarette, out the door, and to the barn while I was still trying to get my eyes open. He was always eager to get going; it was that way until the last long drag from his glowing cigarette after he blew out the oil lamp at night.

His interest in me first began to quicken when I got a letter or two. "Can you read those?" he asked. "Can you write, too?"

He seemed fascinated. Would I write a letter for him, "to a little girl in Mobridge," he asked.

"Prettiest little girl. Last thing she said when I left was 'Be sure to write!' Man, she sure was pretty—hot damn." Al shook his head slightly, remembering how she looked. "Think you could write a letter for me?"

"Sure," I answered. "Tell me what you want to say."

"Aw, I dunno anythin' 'bout letters," he stammered. "You just fix it up the way it's s'posed to sound." Al was quite happy, and added, "I sure will 'preciate it. Little Bird was her name—we called her Birdie."

Little Bird? I thought she must be Indian, or part Indian.

That night I wrote the letter for him and learned he couldn't even sign his name to it. "You go ahead and sign my name," he said. "Then read the whole thing to me."

> Dear Birdie,
>   I think of you often and should have written to you before now. I am working for a Mr. Saunders and am getting along fine. My address is Rt. 4, Box 21, Gannvalley, S.D. If this reaches you, I wish that you would write and tell me about everybody.
>   Love,
>   ALVIN

I had learned that Al's hometown was Mobridge, up in the northern part of the state on the Missouri River. It was so named because of the bridge across the Missouri. Large cattle companies leased Indian lands in the area west of the river. Al's father had been one of the Texans who first brought cattle to the lush grasslands of western South Dakota. It was with the big outfits that Al acquired his training and experience. He was just a wild kid of eleven when he first began to ride for the Drag V, herding on the open range of the Cheyenne River Sioux reservation in 1904. He loved the rough range life and would have stayed after his own father died had he been able to get along with his stepfather.

When I read the letter to him, his face turned crimson as he protested about the "Love." Because of it he thought she wouldn't answer. I managed to convince him she'd like that ending and got the letter ready to mail the next day. Prompted by curiosity, I added a postscript: "Please send me a snapshot of yourself if you have one."

Before I had even mailed it, he asked if there had been a

reply. I explained that his letter had to go by way of St. Paul, and it could take weeks. I dreaded to think of the excuses I would have to make if there were no reply.

But after a few weeks one did come, and Birdie even enclosed a picture of herself and a friend Daisy. The postcard snapshot pleased him and interested me.

"Isn't she pretty?" he said, more to himself than to me.

I thought she was. I had to read her letter to Al so many times I soon knew every word of it:

Dear Alvin,

    We were all glad to hear from you and know that you are well. We thought you were in Texas. Liz is working in a cafe in town, and Little Jim is going to school. He is growing fast and wants to be a cowman like his Pa. Big Jim is with the Millirons outfit on the Moreau. I worked at the Matador headquarters for six months but am home now that Ma died. She died in January. I guess you didn't know. I told Liz I got a letter from you. She wants you to write.

Sincerely,
BIRDIE

I am going with Ray Vivian from Evarts. We might get married this fall.

X X X X

Al and I analyzed nearly every word. "About Texas," he explained, "I really was headed for Texas. That's where I was born—moved up here when I was two. Guess I told you Pa was a cowman. How far is Texas? How long would it take to ride there?" He usually asked two or three questions at a time. Before I had time to reply, or even to half-answer the first, he was asking me to read the next part of the letter.

"Liz is my mother," he went on. "Jim, the bastard! He's my stepfather. My mother is all right. Little Jim is Big Jim's boy. I worked with Big Jim on the Moreau before he and Ma got married. The bastard! He's no good."

Al looked at the page as though he might actually read it. "She really call me 'Dear Alvin'? Where does it say that?" I pointed to the words, and he seemed satisfied.

"The X's mean kisses? Aw—you're being funny now." He skipped over the part about Ray Vivian as though it didn't exist.

He examined the stamp, asked a few questions about the postmark and the postal route, and then handed me the letter and the picture saying he hoped I would write for him again one day. Somehow in the following days he lost interest, and I kept the picture of Birdie and Daisy.

I often entertained Al with my imitations of foreigners, and he was intrigued by the French ones.

"God damn if you don't sound just like a Frenchman!" he exclaimed, insisting on an encore.

Although he laughed almost as heartily at my Italian, Irish, and Swedish imitations, he had no way of knowing if these were good, since he had had contact only with the French.

Al had formed a dislike for Bert, whom he referred to as "The Duke" because of his English background. Bert was in his early thirties, well built, and always modishly attired, bowler hat and all. Al was perhaps jealous of the easy life Bert led, for all he seemed to do around the Saunders place was groom the huge stallion. He regularly put ads in the town paper; tacked up a few posters reading "At Stud, RAJAH, Purebred Percheron, Charles Saunders, Owner," with place and date; and stayed a week at each place before moving on to another town. He had a strange yet sophisticated appearance as he rode through the country on a small horse, purposely used to make the big Percheron look even larger than he was.

One Sunday Bert rode into the ranch wearing a pair of gauntlet gloves I had recently purchased and in which I took great pride. In answer to my objections, he took one off and slapped me lightly across the face with it.

"Do you know what that means in England?" he asked.

"It means the same thing as it does here," I replied, as I jumped in with a left and a right, more in fear than bravery. Whatever the consequences, I felt I had no alternative since several men were looking on.

I was greatly relieved Bert left without a word and did not retaliate, as he looked more than capable of doing. Although he had a weight advantage, he may have been influenced because he had on his good clothes, was not in good physical shape, or felt he was not in friendly territory. Al had shifted his cigarette and was seemingly eager to see a fight or even to participate in one.

Al shook my hand. "You did it, Joe!" Pride and gratitude showed all over him, and Joe was his idea of a short name for George. "You did it! I've been wishing someone would take a pop at 'The Duke.'" After that, he was my friend all the way.

HAYING AND INDIANS

AYING SEASON BEGINS as soon as grass has reached its full growth. Perhaps no work is as persistently hard on a stock ranch as that of working with hay at the hottest time of the year. It begins with the monotonous mowing: sitting on a hard iron seat from daybreak to dark, keeping an eye on the edge of the uncut grass so as not to stray offline, and watching out for rocks while being lulled to unconsciousness by the steady drone of the mower. More than once I dozed off, only to be quickly roused by a nightmare of falling into the cutter.

After the newly cut hay has had several days to dry, there is the backbreaking operation of bucking and stacking it in the fields and building fences around the stacks to keep out the stock. The long hours of hard work required that someone—usually Elsa, the German hired girl, or sometimes Sis—bring a generous quantity of food and drinks halfway between breakfast and dinner, and again in mid-afternoon.

Each day we would take our empty racks and return at noon and night with them filled to overflowing with sweet smelling new-mown hay. Unloading had been simplified by nets of rope which enabled us, with horses, to pull the entire load off the hay-rack beds.

As the haystack grew in height we extended two long ropes over it. By attaching one end of these ropes to the hayrack net, we made a sling whereby the hay was rolled up to form an ever higher mound. Some of the hay in these huge stacks was kept in abeyance as a reserve against dry years.

Haying season is generally a time of fierce thunderstorms, with little warning before great black clouds appear, accompanied by wild wind, pelting rain, terrifying lightning, and resounding crashes of thunder. Water pours out of the sky fast enough to form a vast lake. At times, hailstones as large as hens' eggs pelt the horses into a wild frenzy.

On one particular morning preceded by a hot sunny day, we arrived at our hayfield to be greeted by a sight almost as beautiful as it was unbelievable. Stretched out for over a mile lay a shimmering body of crystal clear water, formed no doubt during the night by rains farther up the valley. Hay, mowers, and other equipment were entirely inundated. In a few days the lake had disappeared, and everything was dried off by hot sun and warming winds, with little or no damage.

In the midst of haying season, a disease known as lumpy jaw struck a few of Saunders's finest steers. The jaw on one side of each animal's face swelled to enormous size. The afflicted animals could not be shipped, so rather than destroy them Mr. Saunders offered them to the Indians. There was no objection to this so long as the steers were not brought onto the reservation or were not moved to where they might infect other cattle. Mr. Saunders permitted the butchering just a short distance from the lane leading to his house so the Indians could get necessary water without going far.

Indians came in droves, new groups arriving as earlier ones finished and left. They brought their papooses and their dogs and set up tepees and racks on which to smoke the meat. Day after day they sat scraping and tanning hides, cutting meat into thin strips which they hung to dry on the barbed wire along the lane. It was a strange sight to see—for half a mile on each side of the lane meat hung from every barb of a four-strand fence! Flies, attracted from everywhere, buzzed all along the fence and around the tepees. Slightly larger pieces of meat hung from poles under which smoky fires were kept going day and night.

Mrs. Saunders, annoyed with the Indians in the yard all the time, refused to stay at the house without a man around. Sis, however, had never expressed any fear. One day she and Elsa, who was horrified of them, were home alone for a short time while I was away on an errand. When I returned, Sis ran to the barn to get me.

"There is an Indian looking into the windows," she cried. "Elsa will just die!"

I hurried out in time to see the Indian, whom I recognized as Crow Splitnose (I had known him from playing ball against the Indian team at Fort Thompson), walk across the garden to the lane. He was said to be one of the survivors of the Massacre at Wounded Knee in December, 1890, considered the last important conflict between Indians and whites in South Dakota and the United States. Splitnose was bitter toward whites because after the battle two hundred Indian men, women, and children and only sixty soldiers lay dead or wounded on the frozen ground.

I decided to have a talk with that Indian and followed him to the encampment. The younger Indians were always quite friendly, but the older ones seemed to hold a grudge toward white men. When I arrived at the camp, Splitnose wasn't in sight, but one of the young men assured me the older Indian meant no harm: "He wanted to see inside the white man's house, since white men looked inside of Indians' tepee."

"Tell the old man to come when Mr. Saunders is home. He will show him inside of house. You no longer come for water when dark or too early morning," I commanded. "You come when men are home."

"Was-tay," he said, "It is well."

The older squaws seemingly took no notice of me as, with heads down, they continued with their work, sharpening knives on field stones, scraping hides, adding more strips of meat to growing piles. Younger women smiled and then continued with their work, digging shallow pits in which to bury the offal. Little boys were chewing on strips of dried meat.

"Ta-lo?" one asked, offering me a piece, which I accepted. "Was-tay"—good—I responded. He smiled, happy.

As days went by, the Indians began to decrease in number, but it was many weeks before the fences were all cleared, the carrion buried, the tepees down, the fires out, and the dogs quiet.

GOOD-BYE TO A FRIEND

S IS OFTEN CAME AROUND while I was grooming the blacks and Molly. There were few girls of her age for miles around, and none so attractive or intelligent. Her capable, educated mother had been able to provide her with better learning than if she had attended the local school. Not neglecting her cultural education, her parents had accumulated a well-stocked library to encourage her reading and had provided piano lessons at the considerable expense of bringing the teacher out regularly from Wessington Springs. Sis's attractiveness was enhanced by her womanly figure, as evidenced by a remark of "Hap" Hooper, one of the men: "She has a rear like a hundred-dollar horse."

Certainly the ranch was not the best environment for a pretty and talented young lady who had so much already and even more possibilities for the future. She wrote poems and items for the Gannvalley paper, belonged to a woman's club, and regularly attended the Congregational Church on the scheduled Sundays the preacher came to the valley.

Only rarely did a girl go away to school, but with Sis, it might be expected. A career for her was not considered, but Mr. Saunders was businessman enough to know that a knowledge of ranch bookkeeping along with some typing would be to his as well as his daughter's advantage. It was therefore suggested to Sis that she go to business school. Sis was enthusiastic about the opportunity and seized it without hesitation. A letter to Mr. Saunders's sister in Sioux City, Iowa, where a choice of two schools existed, brought the prompt reply that Aunt Henrietta would be delighted to have Sis stay in her home.

As the day for her departure drew near, Sis, Elsa, and Mrs. Saunders were busy at the house with last-minute preparations and packing. Mr. Saunders's business had to go on as usual, and suddenly he found out he would not be able to take Sis to the train, for he had to meet the Indian agent at Fort Thompson with regard to the lease of grazing land. I was elected to take Sis to Kimball. Considering who else was available to be the alternate, this was not such a great personal compliment, but I was extremely happy about it.

That evening, after a refreshing dip in the creek, I went to bed early to be rested for the big occasion. Early the next morning I awoke feeling mighty good, not only because I would be with Sis but because seldom did I have the opportunity to get a day off, to drive the blacks for a pleasant ride through the country, and to stroll around town and visit the stores.

When I walked to the pasture to get the horses, a red streak across the soft gray sky marked where the sun would rise. I wanted to run toward it, I felt so good. Meadowlarks sang from atop the fence posts and all around me as I whistled back to them. Dewdrops began to glisten on the curly buffalo grass and spider webs as the sun rose. Although it was the same damp dew I hated each morning when it rendered my shoes and socks a soggy mess, that morning the water droplets appeared to be diamonds.

Before breakfast I gave the horses a careful grooming, washed the buggy, oiled the harness, and brushed the cushions. The glistening yellow wheels, yellow fly nets, and purple velvet cushions were matched for luxury nowhere else in the area. I admired the buggy during the tearful farewell by Sis's mother. Her father gave last minute admonitions about "life in Sioux City," and Elsa supplied a small box of homemade cookies.

Sis had all new clothes and bags. She looked so ladylike in a navy blue suit with white braid trimming. Her high-buttoned shoes were patent leather with white tops that showed beneath her three-quarter-length skirt. Her hat with a small white plume matched the suit. Over her hat she wore a pink scarf which matched her blouse. White cotton gloves and a white bag completed her fashionable outfit.

Mr. Saunders looked at me approvingly as he helped Sis into the buggy. I was wearing new jeans, with cuffs turned up about six inches showing my polished tan boots. My white shirt had a blue collar and cuffs so I wore a blue kerchief around my neck. I had on my gauntlet gloves with the long fringes and a black stockman-style hat.

We were on our way with raucous cries of scattering guinea hens and the barking of the pet collie. Sis retained a quiet calm, which was much in contrast to her usual vivacious demeanor and mischievous deviltry that could be annoying when there was work to be done.

Catching me in the barn, she would sometimes sneak up, let out a yell, jump on my back and pin me to the ground. To this there was no defense, except for one time when I was prepared and threw her over my head. She lay there in the hay, either stunned or pretending to be. I lifted her up, apologizing, and held her gently. Suddenly she sprang loose and was off on a run, calling me names in a display of anger I scarcely knew she could muster. After that she used another tactic, advancing with a boxing or wrestling pose. "Want to box?" she would say, or "Want to hassle?" (She probably meant wrestle.) These rounds usually ended by her calling for help when there was no one around to hear and accusing me of being rough while I was the one who got the bruises. Some day, I thought, she is going to yell bloody murder and someone will hear. That did not seem to bother her, but it made me a little uneasy.

On this trip she was riding along sedately, the lady replacing the brat, but either way she was nice to be with. It was twenty-six miles to Kimball, and we had left in plenty of time to arrive for the noon train. After leaving the valley the blacks went along at a lively pace on the high, flat prairie. The road to Gannvalley and beyond was deserted. We saw one lone cowboy and some cattle. In town we made a brief stop for Sis to pick up her mail. Coming out of the store-post office, she was tucking some letters into her new purse. One was quite noticeably addressed in the Spencerian handwriting of the creamery man she had spoken of the day she drove me to the ranch from Sy's.

A few miles beyond Gannvalley, we began to see farms with neat rows of cut grain in shocks. Corn was at full height, tasseled out and showing ears. We passed a farm wagon or two and also the tandem wagons of the freighter, who waved and greeted Sis with enthusiastic cordiality. As the sun rose higher in the cloudless sky and it grew warm, we slowed our pace. We talked about books she had read, school studies, and Sioux City, which she thought of as being much like Omaha since both cities are on the Missouri River. Her father had told her about the huge packing houses and stockyards and the big grain elevators.

"Tell me about Omaha. What did your father do there?"

I told her Pa had been an agent for a flour mill and how much we had enjoyed hiking along the banks of the river where we picked wild grapes, plums, crab apples, berries, walnuts, hickory nuts, and bitternuts; and visiting the beautiful parks: Krugs, Hanscom, Deer, and Riverview, where we swam in the lake after dark. I described Hayden's, Bennett's, and Brandeis department stores, the big Paxton & Vierling Iron Foundry, the John Deere Plow Company, and the streetcars.

I told her about Storz, Metz, and Krugs breweries and how Krugs had furnished our baseball uniforms and ball field. We had played under their name and traveled to small towns where they owned saloons that were within a day's round trip. After the games, free beer and sumptuous family-type dinners were served at local hotels. When a sudden Midwest storm came up, we got to stay overnight; there was little sleep but much fun. Returning to Omaha in the four-horse-drawn carryall the next day, boys would rush into a roadside farm place to buy fruit and milk but seldom did the farmer or his wife accept pay.

Sis asked more questions. "Tell me about the people, and the schools, and what else you did."

I told her about the German section where we belonged to the gymnastic club Turnverein, the Bohemian section where we competed with the Ted Jed Sokal junior gymnasts, and the Irish part where we went to Mass at St. Patrick's and to Sunday School afterwards. I remembered hearing the roar of the crowds at the ball park across the street where the Omaha team of the Western League played its Sunday games. There were the three Omaha Newspapers my brothers and I had both delivered and sold: the *Bee, World Herald,* and *Daily News.* At Creighton University we had seen many thrilling football games. In the center of town was a big high school that my brother Nick attended and had been a uniformed cadet. I finished by telling her about the theaters, especially describing vaudeville at the Orpheum.

"My, my!" she exclaimed. "Why would one ever leave there? Will you go back? What are your ambitions? Everyone should have an objective."

It was time to change the subject. I had no more objectives at the time than a jaybird. One might have said my ambition went as far as next payday, but even then I didn't get to keep the money.

"What is wrong with this?" I asked, waving my hand to indicate the sweeping, rolling beauty of the prairie and the cultivated farmland. "Nowhere is it more beautiful than right here and now."

"Oh, yes," she interrupted, ignoring my comment, "all you talk about in Omaha is boys. Were there no girls?"

"There sure were," I acknowledged, "but none so pretty as right here. Let's talk about you. You have a nice voice and carry a tune well. Sing some of those songs you play on the piano and sing at home."

We sang them together: "Down by the Old Mill Stream," "In the Shade of the Old Apple Tree," "Napanee," "Juanita," and "Red Wing." The last one was our favorite; we thought we sang it best.

By this time, she was in a mood for stories. My specialty was telling the ones with an Irish brogue which I thought I did well from being around the Irish so much at St. Patrick's. The stories I had heard were mostly from Protestant friends, however, many of whom thought I was Irish because of my associations:

> Policeman: "What's your name?"
> Driver: "It's on the side of me wagon."
> Policeman: "It's obliterated."
> Driver: "Yer a liar. It's O'Brien."

"She is going to marry an Irish lad."
"Oh, really!"
"No—O'Reilly."

To a boy who has been talking with Irish brogue: "I didn't know you were Irish."
Boy: "I'm not. I'm German. My English teacher was Irish."

Pat writes a letter to a friend back home: "I have a foin job here. All I do is carry hod up six flights. There is a fellow up there who does all the work."

Since Sis had heard few of them before, she thought these and more vaudeville jokes and stories were hilarious.

Time passed all too quickly. We reached the station only minutes before the train was due to arrive. Sis, almost tearfully, begged me to take good care of Molly: "Turn her out to pasture while days are warm, stable her nights, curry her and comb out her mane and tail, trim and oil her hoofs, feed her some grain night and mornings." I knew all of that, but she felt better by repeating it.

"Please," she concluded, placing a hand on my arm, "please don't ever permit anyone to ride her." Tears gleamed in her eyes. I could have taken her into my arms.

I assured her I would take good care of Molly, as she boarded the train. I handed her luggage up to her, and we waved good-bye as the train disappeared into the distance, leaving me with an empty feeling. Sis was gone, and tomorrow it would be "back to the hayfield" without her laughter and interruptions.

BACK TO WORK

ON THE WAY BACK to the ranch, I angled off the main road fourteen miles out of Kimball to cut across the prairie for a brief stop at home. I did not get home often as the distance from the Saunders's was more than eleven miles. The three-mile walk from Sy's, though not desirable, at least had been possible on Saturday nights.

I found Nick and Ed working at haying. Their equipment seemed inadequate and on such a small scale compared to what I had become accustomed to on the huge Saunders place.

Both boys looked at my clean clothes and the elegant rig. Sensing that the sight of such luxury could easily cause dissatisfaction with what they had to put up with at home, I offered a sham proposal to trade places with either brother and compared the freedom they had with working long hours for someone else.

Pa appeared and asked, "What kind of work is going on at the ranch now? How are you getting along there?" and a lot of other questions.

Agnes was helping Ma in the kitchen, so I went in to finish my visit there. I could not stay long, as I had to get back to the ranch in time to change my clothes and take care of the horses and buggy before supper. In answer to Ma's question as I left, I told her I did not know when I would get home again.

Haying continued into fall. Haystacks dotted the land on the high prairie and in the lush meadows along the creek. Those stacks that were to remain had to be fenced, and loads of stout pine posts were hauled from town. We dug post holes and strung strong wires secured by long staples. As winter came on, hungry cattle would test them with their full weight while craning their necks, leaving tufts of hair on the barbs in their effort to get a few wisps of food.

Working hours were long, and our bodies ached every night. Most of us were too tired to go into town on Saturday nights, but Al would always go, if only for a short time. One night he won a Winchester twelve-gauge shotgun in a saloon raffle.

We put the gun to good use when we discovered some large buffalo fish temporarily stranded in flood waters after a heavy downpour. Stunning the fish by blasts from the gun, Al was able to get enough so we could enjoy our first fresh fish dinner in a long time, a welcome change after a steady diet of pork. Because of the lack of refrigeration, the weather would have to be colder before we could have beef. Since Al was not a hunter and felt he had no further use for the shotgun, he traded it for some silver inlaid spurs with chains that jangled.

With the arrival of fall, Mr. Saunders was out quite a bit of the time buying cattle. It became my duty to join with Al for two or three days a week to drive them in. Seeing new places, meeting people, and riding a good horse made it a pleasant occupation. We were sometimes invited to a meal or for a drink, but we had to turn down the invitations because of Mr. Saunders's orders.

Al, with his jingling silver spurs, and me, with my long-fringed gauntlet gloves! We might have been with Sir Galahad in search of the Holy Grail, with Cody in the Buffalo Bill Wild West Show, with Teddy Roosevelt at the charge of San Juan Hill! For us, it was sufficient to be known as "one of the Saunders men."

By the end of September haying was finally over; and the crew, one by one, left. I was fortunate to be held over along with Al. Bert had been the first to leave, when the stallion season ended. "The Duke," as we called him, left for his home in Canada with assurance from Mr. Saunders that he could return, if he so wished, at the beginning of the stud season next year. Caring for Rajah, feeding, grooming, and exercising him became one of my duties. It wasn't a particularly desirable chore because, lacking exercise, he often "felt his oats." Rising up on his hind legs to tower above me, he struck at the air. I realized if he ever came down on me with those huge iron-clad hoofs, it would be painful, to say the least.

In late October a few snow flurries and frost at night warned of the approaching winter. However, recurrences of Indian summer continued into November, bringing a few days or even a week of calm and warm air with nearly cloudless skies. Prairie fires in the distance added their smoke to the hazy atmosphere on the horizon.

By Thanksgiving Day water holes began to freeze over, and throughout the winter we had to chop through the ice to keep them open. Hay had to be spread for the hungry steers being held over through the winter. Most of the birds had migrated south during September and October. Only the hardy barnyard sparrows remained, nestled in the many holes they had made in the sides of the haystacks. Prairie chickens congregated in coveys of fifty or more, feeding on grain or seeds, with their inevitable sentry atop a haystack to warn of impending danger. Their roosts at night were holes excavated in the snow, which by late November was appearing layer upon layer. All the signs of winter had become evident, but days of bitter cold were sometimes followed by several almost as warm as spring.

As December progressed, everyone began to anticipate Christmas. Charlie Saunders and his wife looked forward to the time Sis would arrive home for her mid-term two-week vacation, filling the house with her laughter and music. Mrs. Saunders was busy getting Sis's room ready with winter blankets and fresh curtains. Al had little to look forward to and seemed not to care. He would be kept busy caring for the horses and hauling and scattering hay on the prairie for the stock. No doubt the Saunders would provide a good dinner including cigars and toddies; in town there would be stronger drinks. For me, it would be home for a few days, and I eagerly looked forward to being with my family.

PRAIRIE CHRISTMAS

THE MORNING of December twenty-third, I set out for home across the snow-covered prairie on Eagle Chief, the bay gelding I rode when going after cattle for Mr. Saunders. He was a good horse but the years of twisting, turning, sudden stopping, and reversing as a stock horse had taken their toll. Eagle Chief's spavined legs, stiffened further by the cold, caused him to limp at first; but once we were on the road he was again his old self, mincing his way down icy slopes, avoiding drifts. He knew the prairie so well I turned him toward home and gave him his head.

Because of a late start and the slow travel, I arrived at noon and found the family at dinner in the kitchen.

Greeting me, Pa noted, "You've grown, filled out."

Serving my plate of boiled beef and vegetables, Ma expressed anxiety that the food might not be so good as the kind I had become accustomed to. I quickly reassured her that after my morning ride no other meal could be better.

Agnes, saying nothing, looked at me with wonder throughout the meal as though I were a stranger.

The Christmas season had brought the usual abundance of mail from relatives. It was read with even greater delight because this year we were so very far away from all of them. A letter from Aunt Mary, Ma's older sister who with Uncle Theis and their children lived on a prosperous farm near Plainview, Nebraska, recalled the grand vacation we had spent there one summer. She enclosed the usual picture of their farm and their ever-increasing herd of cows. Aunt Rose, whose farm in Minnesota we had also visited, wrote that she, Uncle Will, and cousins Florence and Joe planned to move to Texas. Plattsmouth postmarks indicated letters from Grandpa and from Uncle Pete who, with his family, lived on a farm adjoining Grandpa's, the old homestead where Ma was born.

Uncle Nick, the prosperous owner of the flour mill in Weeping Water, Nebraska, for whom Pa had been the Omaha agent, expressed interest in our progress in South Dakota and included news of Aunt Anna's social activities, cousin Mary's new interest in dramatics and accomplishments in violin and piano, and cousin George's athletic ability on high school football and baseball teams.

Uncle George, "the sourdough" whom we remembered so well for stories of his adventures in the Yukon, and Aunt Tinie were in California where he was trying, with little success, to sell Ford autos. Uncle Joe, youngest of the Holmes family, had recently married and moved onto a farm in Arkansas.

Pa had received the wishes of "Froeliche Weinachten" from his brother and many nieces and nephews in Germany. Some had sent photographs; but their letters, in German script, caused Pa some difficulty in translating.

Nick, who wrote a beautiful Spencerian hand, corresponded

with Della Waters, a second cousin whom we had never met, in St. Helena, California. He had written one of his usual long letters and received an equally interesting one from her with glowing accounts of California, the Napa Valley in particular, and a set of pictures: The Old Bale Mill, The Stone Bridge, grape vineyards and fruit orchards, wooded scenes along the highway, the geysers, and Mt. St. Helena. A nostalgic letter for Agnes arrived from her Omaha chum Hermenia Leighleiter, expressing hope they might someday be together again.

Ed and Agnes were eager to talk about the Lyon Township Public School, a typical one-room schoolhouse, where their world centered around teacher, playmates, games, pictures, and books. They were delighted when Nick suggested we hitch a team to the sleigh and ride over there.

Near the humble building, the big snowman they had taken days to build stood guard, with battered hat, old scarf, pipe, and broom in hand. Leading us to the unlocked door, Ed quickly ushered us inside and eagerly announced, "All the decorations are being left until we return after vacation." Chains of colored paper festooned the room, and Christmas drawings covered the blackboard.

Teachers had come and gone to the little barbed-wire enclosed schoolhouse where grades were determined only by the "reader." With important work to be done on the farms, few scholars had reached the *Eighth Reader,* the accomplishment necessary to receive a diploma. Ed and Agnes praised their first teacher, a nineteen-year-old graduate of Carlisle Indian School in Pennsylvania; "He was fun and a good horseman—a real bronco buster!" Before the end of the term, he left and was followed by a niece of Mr. Balster, the school trustee whose family always boarded the teacher. A pleasant young woman with a deformed arm, she had probably accepted the post in order to complete her own grammar school education. She left to marry the young immigrant blacksmith in Gannvalley. Their current teacher was Miss Budlong, a buxom blonde from Minnesota who was enthusiastic about her first teaching position. In addition to seeing that the schoolroom was neat and clean, she had been responsible for an ingenious Nativity scene constructed with cutouts, cardboard, and watercolors. The scene was extended with colored chalk half the length of the blackboard, where far in the distance the three wise men were shown being guided by a silver star.

In answer to my question about attendance, Agnes said there were ten pupils, but added, "Most don't attend regularly." Of the pupils, the one who had to travel the greatest distance was Carrie Clayton, a small pale girl of fourteen who rode an old sway-backed farm horse from her home which was south and across Smith Creek. Carrie had gotten lost in a blizzard the previous winter and caused much consternation until she was found. The two younger Burians to the west did not live a great distance but had to go around a wash and a coulee; the fact that only Bohemian was spoken in their home further hampered their learning. Ed and Agnes, a good mile and a half north of the school, seldom missed a day, perhaps as much for Pa's desire for "peace around the place," as for their education. The four Balster girls and their younger brother, to the east, were half of the class. School began when they and the teacher appeared in an old spring wagon; if the wind was right, their singing and shouts could be heard before they came over the rise.

Ed said he had heard attendance was better than ever this term and that classes had never been so large before. Even the older Burian boys Frank and Antone, as well as Gus and Tador Runge, had decided to brush up on their studies. It was reported that Miss Budlong, however, "being true to a young man back home," had refused all dates.

Early the next morning Ed and I rode horseback to Vega for a few purchases and the mail. Ma was planning a Christmas dinner and had given us a list of items needed. There had been more snow during the night. We avoided the drifts and the snow-covered roads and kept to windblown higher ridges where we could. Ed's Prince, a small husky dog of mixed breed, followed closely behind.

It was still early when we got to Vega. The town was deserted except for one sleigh and team at the hitching pole in front of Fousek's store. A shotgun leaned against the seat, and a large freshly killed rabbit lay on an old blanket.

"Wonder whose sleigh that is?" asked Ed, as we dismounted. Peering through a clear place in the frost-covered window before we entered the store, he answered his own question. "It's 'Big' Sobek's. He's the oldest Sobek, and one *tough guy!*"

Inside the store, Big was hacking open a case of chewing tobacco. Although he was not a tall man, he did look big in his sheepskin-lined coat. He was a broad person with an inch or more of black beard, and he seemed even bigger because of his loud voice that could be heard all over. Ed said Big lived some-where beyond the Crow reservation and that in spite of reports he had a wife and a bunch of kids Ed didn't know anyone who had met them. His reputation included a mean disposition that had reportedly caused him trouble. As we passed, there was no greeting, for Big was one of those characters if you don't greet first, "t' hell with you."

Quiet, meek Mrs. Fousek waited on us. We bought oranges, apples, some hard Christmas candies—a round kind cut from brightly-colored sticks with flowers and other small designs in the white centers, and a striped variety fluted, twisted, and pleated—and some peppermints, Pa's favorite. Mrs. Fousek gave Ed one of the large wooden pails that the candy came in, noting there were a lot of crumbs still stuck in the bottom. Ed filled it with our purchases and hung it at the side of his saddle.

Upon arriving home, we realized Prince was nowhere in sight. As an hour or more passed we wondered what could have happened to him, for he had never strayed before. We finally saw him coming slowly over the rise in the road, stopping to rest occasionally. Forager that he was, we knew he had to be dragging something. With his rest periods becoming more frequent we went out to meet him and found, to our dismay, that Prince was dragging a rabbit almost as large as himself.

"Big's rabbit!" Ed exclaimed, knowing Prince had never been able to catch one. Could he possibly have dragged Big's rabbit out of the sleigh and all that distance?

Ed was terrified. "Big's a tough guy. He'll kill us if he thinks we stole his rabbit. There'll be a trail in the snow—blood spots and dragging marks. I expect we'll see his sleigh any minute. Big'll storm in here with fire in his eyes, teeth showing through that beard—he won't give us a chance to explain."

We could do nothing but wait. The rabbit remained in plain sight; hiding it would have been useless. As the long min-utes passed, no horses, no sleigh, and no Big appeared. Ed finally stopped looking down the road. "Do you think he's accused some-one else?"

I shrugged my shoulders. We often wondered, but never heard.

Jimmy Havlik had heard I was coming home and dropped in around noon to invite Nick and me to the Bohemians' Christ-mas Eve party that night at the hall above his uncle's store in

Vega. It was more or less a family affair, a party of such gaiety that only the Bohemians could put on. The evening began with a Christmas Nativity play, staged by the children in appropriate costumes, after which they each stood in line to receive an orange, an apple, and a bag of "candies." Games for the small children were directed by one of the teachers who had been invited, and everyone else danced to accordion music, continuous and in increasing tempo. How they danced, on and on, round and round: folk dances, square dances, the schottische, and polkas!

Mrs. Havlik, Jimmy's mother, who had boasted of having had "fifteen children, seven living, all without benefit of doctor or midwife," and who always complained of her ills and told of her gall bladder operation at the Mayo Clinic in Rochester, Minnesota, entered the polka contest. Urged and cheered by friends, the contestants danced on and on. The accordion player showed signs of tiring, and one couple after another dropped out until only Mrs. Havlik and her partner Joe Urban, a strong young man, remained. Spinning around in the middle of the floor, they became the center of attraction. Enjoying the attention, they continued, encouraged by friends and disregarding some pleas to stop. At last, one of the older men placed his arms around the accordion player, forcing him to stop the music. Mrs. Havlik stood glassy-eyed, too dizzy to walk, and had to be helped from the floor.

"Why did you stop us?" she complained indignantly, feeling heroic perhaps, knowing she had won with a great show.

The party was lively, and the generally shy Bohemian girls were friendly and good mixers, probably because they felt at ease with their own group and since most of the families were related. The pretty girls were neatly, if not modishly, attired in dresses they had made themselves. Their hands, however, were rough and coarse, for they worked in the fields along with the men. Almost without exception, the girls and their sturdy, equally handsome brothers were good dancers.

Rosie Kovanda, one of the less popular girls and quite naive, seemed extremely happy, for some of the boys arranged a mock fight over her. They went outside to have it out and came back with clothes disarranged and faces smudged. She and many others thought it was real; those of us who knew would *never* give it away. By the time the evening ended, we had danced at least briefly with all the girls: Jimmy Havlik's sisters Mary, Annie, and Stacey; the two Fousek girls Emma and Fannie; Mary Plos, Emma Burian, Annie Pitsek, Katie Simek, Lydia Jika, and a number of others. Nick enjoyed himself more than usual, particularly because he seldom went anywhere when I was not home.

A late supper was the final festivity. Coffee, made in a large blue enameled pot on top of the potbellied stove, was served with rich cream and sugar. The Bohemians apparently liked lots of cream. Along with pies and cakes, there were more kolaches (a Bohemian pastry) than one could eat. The happy, gay atmosphere continued as folks bundled up their sleepy children and headed home.

The next day was Christmas, different from the ones we had enjoyed in Omaha. Months of country living had made us all hearty eaters, and we insisted on big country style meals with lots of cream gravy, root vegetables such as parsnips and rutabagas, home-canned corn, tomatoes, homemade pickles, and mince and pumpkin pies. Winter was the season for an abundance of fresh pork and beef; we did our own butchering and had it at its cheapest and best. Ma made sausages, head cheese, blutwurst, knockwurst, sauerkraut—all the German dishes she had been raised on. She pickled cucumbers and watermelon rind and made piccalilli. We had plenty of all the things we could grow. Ma added cranberries and assorted nuts from the general store and put together one of the best Christmas dinners to be had anywhere.

In the evening Nick and I got out the sled, hitched up the team, and drove toward Lyonville to see the Balster family, where the chief attraction was the four pretty girls. Mr. Balster very kindly greeted us and quickly disappeared. He was a good man who usually avoided people, perhaps because of a sensitivity about his appearance. His nose, chin, and one thumb had been shot off when his young son accidentally pulled the trigger of a shotgun the father was holding. A heavy black beard hid some of the scars.

The Balsters' large home reflected both refinement and femininity. Nora, about eighteen, and Alberta, near sixteen, both played the piano well and entertained us with music, stereoscopic slides, games, and delicious food including a variety of homemade candies and Christmas cookies. I also got to meet Miss Budlong, the school teacher, who had been accepted as one of the Balster family; she was everything Ed had said: vivacious, witty, and attractive.

The Balster girls had the verve and glow of abundant good health and the beauty of rustic simplicity. Their voices were soft, and their manner easy and gentle. Though they were good company and nice to be with, both were almost too proper to be interesting as sweethearts but, no doubt, would make good mates someday for any man wanting a perfect farm wife.

After an enjoyable evening, Nick and I went to get our team and sled and found to our dismay they were gone. We could not even guess which direction Dick, the habitual runaway, would have headed.

Rather than let our fair hostesses know of our carelessness in not fastening our horses properly, we struck out for home on foot. Our light shoes and good clothes were scarcely the type one would choose for a winter hike through the snow. The two-mile walk afforded ample opportunity to consider the eruption this episode would cause at home.

When we arrived, the packed snow showed no trace of the horses' return. Before starting for the house I decided, in spite of cold wet feet, to look around. Luckily, in spite of the dark, I saw a shadow. The horses were standing with sled intact wedged between a haystack and a shed some distance from the barn. Our "merry Christmas," if not ruined, would certainly have been badly marred had it been necessary to report to Pa the loss of team and sled!

The following day, before I left to return to the Saunders ranch, Ma served the rabbit. She had marinated it with a little vinegar and a touch of spices. Of all the special foods Ma ever cooked, her rabbit, hunter style, was the best. Ed, however, still fearing that Big Sobek would get him, had little appetite.

TREACHEROUS MISSION

THE DAYS FOLLOWING my return from the brief holiday vacation at home were not extremely busy. My duties were light and without much ranch work other than the normal winter routine and daily chores. Sis was still home, but I didn't see much of her, mainly glimpses each morning and evening as she left and returned either riding Molly or with her mother in the cutter which had replaced the buggy for the winter. Our conversation was limited to greetings and reports of Christmas, without time for a real discussion of Sioux City and her school life. With so many friends and invitations, coupled with the advantage of pleasant weather, she was seldom home.

Unseasonably warm temperatures had continued for several days, and Mr. Saunders thought it a good time to have me take a two-year-old Hereford bull to a buyer in Kimball. The next morning we had the big pink-eyed, white-faced, curly-haired fellow loaded before the sun began to throw its golden rays across the silvery hard surface that had resulted from the alternate melting and freezing of the snow. Horses that had been in the barn too long were eager to go. With the roads slick and smooth as glass, we made good time.

After delivering the bull, I figured there was enough time for a hearty meal at Emma's Restaurant, a visit with Gus Sobek at his saloon, and a haircut.

Emma, who had "proved up" on her homestead, was now living the easy life, preparing three meals a day and waiting on tables while swapping stories with traveling salesmen.

"Howdy, Puncher," she greeted me. "How's tricks in the sticks? Thought you was snowed in. How come you're in town?" She busied herself stirring up the stew without waiting for an answer.

I tarried over cups of hot coffee at Emma's and spent too much time at the saloon with Gus, whose folks had had a cattle ranch out our way that he liked to talk about. A chilly wind had risen, and I decided to skip the haircut and went on to the livery stable where the man greeted me, "I'm told you're a Saunders man. Sure glad to see you!"

He told me about a young woman and her baby stranded at the Kimball House. "Her husband bought a piece of land not far from Gannvalley and was building a cabin. She wrote a letter telling him she was coming and that he should meet her, but she's been here two weeks now with no sign of him. She has no money and no way to reach him, so what can she do?" He shrugged his shoulders, adding, "You take her out. She'll give you directions on how to get there."

"Listen, Fella," I said quickly, "she and nobody else can tell anyone how to get there because there's no road. I don't think I could find it myself, and I've been there. If it were summer, I might take a chance. You're talking about Schulty, aren't you?"

"Yeh, that's him. Know him?" he asked eagerly.

"Well, I've met him," I admitted. "He's the only one building a shack out that way."

I remembered Fred Schulty. One Sunday in Vega when he was getting supplies he had stopped to watch us practicing for our ball game. After he had tossed a few and taken a turn at bat, we termed him "a good prospect," and he promised to play with us. When he didn't show up, two of us went out to his place. One look and it was obvious there would be no days off for him for a long time! He was busy with hammer and nails finishing a shed for the horses. Nearby was a pile of lumber for the cabin. He needed a well and a windmill, but first a dam. In reply to our comments, he said he was also going to do some plowing and put in a crop. "I'm trying to get things in shape," he told us, "so I can send for my wife. She's staying with her folks in Iowa until after the baby arrives."

We looked at the land, rough and strewn with volcanic rock, not even good grazing. I thought of it as one of Sy's coyote hunting places, fit for jackrabbits and buzzards. Knowing Iowa was noted for rich soil, tree-lined roads, and prosperous farms, I asked Schulty how he had decided to buy the place.

"I read an ad in our newspaper: 'Farm in Beautiful Gann-valley.' Offered an all-expense paid trip." He needed to say no more. We knew the story—an extravagant description, food and lodging in Kimball, cigars and drinks, a visit by fast team to the good farms along the creek bottom, a hard sell, and a fast close with a substantial down payment.

"What do they ask for this land?" we inquired.

"I paid twenty-five dollars an acre," he replied.

We didn't tell him we knew similar land could be bought for a dollar or less. We wished him well and said we were sorry he coudn't play baseball.

"Maybe next season," he had said good-naturedly as we left.

The stableman was continuing his story. "This woman, I tell you, has no money. Mrs. Conant is keeping her out of the goodness of her heart. She's been there since the week before Christmas. Can't get in touch with her husband, and no one has come in from out that way. You're the first we've seen. Besides you know where he lives, so you'll take her out, won't you? Mrs. Conant will sure appreciate it, too. She ain't chargin' her a cent."

"How can I?" I protested. "I work for Mr. Saunders. The team isn't mine. It's miles off the traveled road. Ever been out that way? I doubt that a sled can get through. It's rough country, boulders."

The man went on, undaunted. "I know Charley Saunders. He always puts up here. He won't mind," he insisted.

There were a few flakes of snow in the air, and the wind was colder.

"No, I wouldn't think of it. No chance!"

"Well, at least, you will go over and talk to her. Surely, you'll do that, and tell her you met her husband?"

"All right." I consented to do that much.

We assembled in Mrs. Conant's little parlor, since the Kimball House had no lobby or public parlor. Mrs. Schulty was a slender, pale, shy young woman of no more than twenty; so very different from the rugged homesteader women that one couldn't help feeling sorry for her. It was going to be a rough life, and I wanted no part in it.

Mrs. Conant and the stableman begged; Mrs. Schulty sobbed pitifully; and the baby cried and cried. It was all too much. Begging turned to pleading, and I finally gave in.

In a hurry to get started because of the weather, I had my team at the door within minutes. Mrs. Conant waved from the doorway. I waited and continued to wait, anxiously now. I went inside, got too warm, and went out again. Everything about this trip was contrary to my better judgment. It was growing cold. The horses became restless. Finally I buckled the blankets on them and went inside once more. My heavy winter clothes and the anxiety brought on a sweat. Again I went out and got colder than ever; the wind seemed to get stronger. Would a woman take a bath before going out in such weather, I wondered, as I tried to think what could possibly be keeping her. What could be taking so long? Did she have to pack? I had assumed she was ready.

Finally she appeared, seemingly taking her own sweet time, but perhaps she wasn't capable or didn't know how to move faster. She called for me to carry her bags, heavy ones, probably filled with knickknacks for the new home, I decided.

Placing her and the baby on clean hay in the corner of the sleigh box, I wrapped them with the warm horse blankets. By the time we had gone east to cross the railroad track and had turned north into the open road, it was snowing hard. The wind grew in intensity and it continued to grow colder. The snow turned to sleet and, lashed by the gale, stung my face. My eyes watered and frosted to slits. To keep warm, I attempted to run alongside the sled but had to give that up because the snow was deep and rough and there was danger of falling. The baby slept, and Mrs. Schulty remained quiet except to ask if we were nearly there. We were less than a third of the way! Another long pause, and she began to whimper. She didn't know it, but she hadn't experienced anything yet! When we turned off the main road onto the open flat, the sled slithered and swayed. Some sharp jolts came from the rim rocks. On the hogback we were caught in the open wind. Where the snow had been swept clean, the sled tipped at perilous angles.

My feet were freezing! They were already numb and without feeling so that I found it difficult to keep from falling. I had to disregard caution and good judgment and act only in desperation, for we would have to make a run for it. My hands were useless; but with the reins wrapped around my wrists, I managed to guide the horses as I urged them on. Avoiding large rocks and holes required all the attention and skill at my command. There were smaller rocks, sharp and dangerous outcroppings. The runners scraped some of them, and the sleigh box tilted crazily. I had no time for thought of a runner collapsing, a whiffletree snapping, a strap breaking, or a horse stumbling and falling.

There were no landmarks to judge by; no houses, no trees. The only time I had approached the cabin was from another direction. With the fierce wind swirling the snow about, I could not be sure whether I was holding the proper course, nor could I be sure of what we were headed for.

Just as my doubts became greatest, I saw a farm through the graying dusk. My moment of joy diminished as we drew nearer. It was a cabin all right, and I recognized the shedlike barn; but there was no sign of life. No light shone from the window, and even worse, no smoke rose from the chimney. I tried to shout but wasn't sure that I heard my voice—it must have trembled at the sight of a cold, deserted cabin standing out there in the frozen nowhere.

I was almost without hope, but the door opened and I realized there was a man in the doorway. Schulty came out, staring wide-eyed and gaping, speechless, as he recognized his wife.

"What—what—are you doing here?" he managed to stutter.

She handed him the baby. Neither spoke. He was so stunned that he could neither think nor act.

"Blanket the horses," I begged. "Build a fire, heat some water."

Gathering his thoughts, he began to do these tasks as though in a trance. As he tried to coax a fire in the little stove, he explained he had no fuel other than the shavings and scraps from the lumber. Smoke puffed around the stove lids, lay there, and was sucked back up again.

"Have you some whiskey?" I inquired.

He had none.

"Coffee, then?"

None of that either.

"I'll make tea," he decided, dipping water from a pail of melted snow that had started to freeze over. As the water heated, man and wife became aware of each other's presence and gradually started to talk.

"Why didn't you let me know that you were coming?" he began.

"I wrote to you over a month ago," she said, tearfully. "I wanted to be with you for Christmas." The holiday was now almost a week past.

"You know that I can't get into town," he explained. "Being off the road here, I can't get through, even when some of the others can."

There was an embarrassing silence.

After much hot tea and arm and leg movements to restore circulation, I began to feel pain in my feet and hands. It was a good sign that frost had not penetrated so deeply as I had feared. It was dark, and I still had considerable distance to go. I heard the wind shriek along the icicled eaves of the little cabin and shuddered. At least I would have the protection of the blankets warmed by the horses.

Headed for home and once on the main road, there was no need to guide the horses. Their instinct made my return to the ranch possible.

I sat in the Saunders's kitchen for hours with my feet and hands in dishpans of snow and water. As life returned, they began to swell, with the pain continuing and getting worse. Whiskey put me to sleep that night and for most of the next day. Mr. Saunders, who often drank alcohol, did not approve of it for treatment; but Al, who had gone some distance to the nearest neighbor to get it for me, insisted there was nothing better for frostbite. By the time my head cleared, I realized I would be confined to my bunk for a few days, perhaps a week, or even two.

Mr. Saunders had a right to be angry but gave his tacit approval of what I had done. He, Mrs. Saunders, and others came into the room to visit. Sis came along with Elsa, who would "straighten up the place." Sis had a lot of candy left over from Christmas and was very generous with it, besides bringing ample supplies of books so I could select the ones I wanted to read.

After one of her visits, Al came in and sniffed the air. "Damned if she hasn't been here again! That little splittail sure as hell likes you."

"Sure does!" I agreed. "She is crazy about me. Some day we are going to pack up all of our worldly goods and move into the big house at the top of the big rock candy mountain. It's too bad that you can't read fairy tales! Sis can have anything, anybody, anytime—you name it, she has it! She probably has a fella in Sioux City."

"O.K., but I still say she likes you," he concluded.

Secretly, I hoped he was right. I was glad Sis returned to Sioux City to finish her business course before my bandages were removed, for there was an unpleasant odor of gangrene and arnica. My toes were swollen and red, with loosened toenails—the ones on the big toes came off. My hands seemed to have made the best recovery and had returned to normal, but the ear that had been windward shriveled like a dried apricot. Everywhere skin continued to peel off, layer after layer, even into spring and summer. Itching and chilblains bothered me for about a year or so.

PROBLEMS WITH THE PEDDLER

WITH THE FIRST warm days, melting snow formed knee-deep muck around the corral, signalling the end of winter. No longer would we shovel drifts and struggle against a cold north wind. After a few more freezes and thaws, we knew it was really spring. Trees along the creek began to bud, and I thought of Fanny's place with wild plum, Juneberry, and wild roses—how beautiful her little lake must be in springtime!

Blue skies with fleecy clouds were marked by long, loose,

wavering lines of Canadian honkers. Their distant "ker-honk" grew louder until, at last, their lead-gray feathers and white cheek patches became visible. In the cornfield a short distance up the road, flocks often broke flight. Cupping their wings, feet outstretched, they came down like falling leaves, their noisy, excited calls continuing as they settled down.

Sis, too, had settled down. She had completed her business course and was home from school, more mature and with the notable changes a few months in the city usually bring. I missed her tomboy antics in the barn. Putting to use methods learned in business school, she typed letters and set up a bookkeeping system for her father, who had previously trusted to his quite remarkable memory. He had never needed to keep books, for he knew the financial standing of everyone in Brule and Buffalo counties; he owed no one, and no one owed him.

I saw Sis only on those evenings Mr. Saunders shared his newspapers with me, the weekly *Kimball Graphic* and the Sunday *Chicago Tribune* which arrived the same day. He and I sat on opposite sides of the oilcloth-covered table in a room just off the kitchen. The coal oil lamp glowed between us as the rancher looked over the prices of livestock, drank black coffee, and smoked his curved pipe. The strong black English tobacco he used was raised in a plot at the side of the house. When his pipe went out, as it often did, he would relight it from the coal oil lamp by using one of the long sticks he had split from a pine board. Pinching out the flame each time had caused large calluses on his thumb and forefinger. The librarylike atmosphere was disturbed only by the periodic bang of his fly swatter. Annoyed by the countless flies that cover the screen doors on stock farms and buzz around the rooms, he would soak lumps of sugar in the alcohol he used to lace his coffee. When flies became groggy, he would smash them with the swatter, cry "Got 'em!" and add an admonition to me, such as, "Let that be a lesson to you on the evils of alcohol."

Perhaps the light of our lamp actually was brighter, as Sis claimed, so she took a place at the end of the table, put her feet up on the bench beside me, and busied herself with her embroidery. As she made cross-stitches and French knots, I mischievously removed one of her dainty slippers. Since she raised no objection, I removed the other and stroked her feet and ankles. Her face remained expressionless as she continued her fancywork. Finally she put on her slippers and left without so much as a "good night."

We went through the same routine the next week, and the next. Since there was no sign of recognition from Sis, I no longer cared to continue the reading sessions. The following week I got the papers after Mr. Saunders had finished with them, took them to the bunkhouse, and read them to Al. I didn't see Sis after that, and it seemed we ignored each other, but I did think about her sometimes.

One evening not long thereafter Al and I were at the pump washing up for supper and a peddler's wagon came down the lane and stopped in the yard.

"It's that fancy Dan again," said Al, "the Syrian that sells stuff for the ladies—ribbons, lace, perfumes, buttons, silk underwear. I see him in town on Saturday nights." The peddler was of medium build, dark, with a small black mustache, and rather good looking. After caring for his horses, he walked up to the house and went inside as though he lived there.

"His name is Stamatis," Al explained further. "He's been coming here for overnight stops with the Saunders for I don't know how long—I guess ever since Sis was a little girl."

I wanted to see the wagon, and Al agreed he wouldn't mind looking inside, too. A quick inspection showed rows of pull-out drawers on each side of an aisle. Steps at the rear folded down for entrance. The wide cushioned seat in front could serve as a bed. On it lay copies of the *Police Gazette,* a weekly printed on glossy pink paper and found in most saloons and barber shops. Devoted to sports and the stage, it contained full page pictures of prize fighters and show girls in tights.

That night, after I was asleep, I became conscious of a flicker of light reflected on the wall inside the bunkhouse. This could have been frightening, but I found it came from a lantern being carried about inside the peddler's wagon. As I looked, Sis emerged carrying something in her arms. The peddler, I assumed, was the source of the ribbons and perfumes Sis used in profusion.

At the barn the following morning, I spoke to the peddler: "You work late."

"That's my business," he replied, obviously offended.

"Nice business," I said. That was all, and he walked away hurriedly.

The next day, after the peddler had left, Mr. Saunders was ready to leave on his scheduled business for the day when he handed me a check. "We won't be needing you any more," he said.

By that time he was already in his buggy, seemingly anxious to get away. I held him back with a request for an explanation.

He was hesitant in his replies: "Yes, your work has been satisfactory, very good in fact. . . . No, it isn't because of a lack of work," which I already knew, for we were coming into the busy spring season.

"Then what is it?" I persisted.

Seemingly reluctant, he turned to bluntness, stating, "You didn't use good judgment in your discussion with Mr. Stamatis about my daughter. She is to blame for bringing it about." He seemed angry as the words came out.

My trying to assure him that there had been no discussion about Sis was to no avail. My offers to confront the Syrian, Greek, or whatever he was, brought out the information: "He won't be back either." That was no consolation to me!

There was no alternative but to prepare to leave. As I packed my few belongings, I thought I should leave a note for Al but remembered he wouldn't be able to read it.

I stopped at the house to say good-bye to Mrs. Saunders. The few times we had spoken she had always been pleasant and had been kind to me when I was laid up with my frostbitten feet. Elsa suggested I wait until Sunday to leave because she would be going to church in Kimball with the Odopahls and they could give me a ride home. I thanked her but told her I preferred to leave that day.

"Eleven miles is a long walk," she said. "Wait a minute, and I'll get some cookies for you to eat on the way."

Sis was nowhere about, much to my regret; I had hoped at least to tell her good-bye.

It was a long walk home—a very long walk. A thousand lighted lamps seemed to be going out one by one. I felt I was leaving the best job I had ever had, and I did not look forward to arriving home under these circumstances.

HOME AGAIN

❖

SODBUSTING A NEW FIELD

I F HOME IS WHERE THE HEART IS, I never made it. After the
initial surprise of seeing me walk dejectedly up the lane,
Pa seemed satisfied with my statement, "I was fired" and a
brief account of what had brought it about. The check I handed
him, no doubt, softened the reaction I had expected.

As far as the farm was concerned, I had been home only a
short time when I sensed the disenchantment that had overtaken
the family. Pa simply wasn't a farmer, never would be, and didn't
know how to get out of it. Moreover, he was not compatible with
our Bohemian neighbors who, though good-hearted, well-meaning
people, just were not his kind. Ma was still making a flimsy pre-
tense that we were farmers in the same sense as her parents in
Nebraska.

I knew Pa would miss the money I had been sending home,
but he didn't show it. I soon learned he was thinking about all
the work I could take over around the place: the tasks he had
been doing or had neglected to do. In his imagination, he had
been working hard.

One day I overheard him talking to Ma: "Why should I have
to work now that the boys are grown? With Ed's help, George and
Nick can take care of the crops, the animals, and everything we
have going now."

I had thought of a better plan, and this seemed the time to
broach it. "Pa, you know the quarter section up the road," I
began, as I walked into the kitchen, "you know where the schoolhouse is?" He nodded, and I continued, "Land under plow is

worth so much more than virgin prairie. If I put that into crops, the result would be better than if I work somewhere else for wages."

Pa didn't think much of my idea, but Nick, who now made almost all the rules regarding the fields and crops, agreed it was the thing to do. Pa held out by refusing to buy a breaking plow. We owned only the ordinary farm plow suitable for Nick's use in fields already cultivated. Breaking the prairie required a special, sturdier plow, the invention of which earned John Deere credit as one of the men instrumental in the opening of the West.

Tador and Gus Runge came over the following Sunday. Hearing my plight, they looked at each other, faces lighting up, with Tador speaking first: "What about ours? Maybe it could be fixed up."

Gus explained theirs had been discarded several years earlier since they no longer had use for it, and it was behind their barn. "Want to come over and look at it now?" he asked. The three of us rushed off eagerly.

We found the plow almost completely covered by weeds. Dragging it out, we saw it was rusted over.

"There's a crack in the beam," observed Gus. "The clevis pin is missing. The colter and shares are dull."

Tador thought Caleb Cummings might be able to fix it even though it was in bad shape. If there was any hope at all, I was willing to haul it to Caleb's place to find out what repairs would put it in working condition.

Caleb and his brother John lived in a tar paper and tin shack under a cutbank along Smith Creek where the stream had long ago changed its course, leaving a crescent-shaped strip of alluvial bottom soil. The rest of the Cummings homestead was rocky, windblown, almost worthless land on the benchland behind the cutbank. The two men, both in their early forties, had a few hogs, a cow, chickens, a small corn field, a thriving garden, and plenty of fish in the creek. They also had a forge, brought with them from their former home where Caleb had been a blacksmith.

I never met John, but Caleb was the dirtiest, most sullen and frightening human I had ever seen, blending in perfectly with the shack and the junk-strewn yard. As he worked in complete silence, I felt his almost colorless eyes glancing at me too frequently through the tousled hair that hung beneath his greasy cap. The time went slowly. Long after I thought he had finished, he kept working—on and on, here and there, a little more hammering, back into the forge and flame, and more hammering. At last he finished—two plowshares sharp as knives, steel straps riveted onto the cracked beam, a new colter, and a clevis pin.

Pleased with the fine result, I fearfully asked his price, thinking it would surely be plenty. He stood there mulling it over in his mind, his heavy lips moving slowly.

"A dollar," he said. There were no more words, and when I paid him, no "thank you" and no "good-bye." What a strange character, I thought as I left.

I saw him only once after that, many weeks later, when I returned to have the plowshares sharpened. In the meantime Gus and Tador, the only ones who seemed to know the Cummings brothers, had told me the almost unbelievable story that both Caleb and John had married. The girls were mail-order brides who had answered their ads in a matrimonial paper. John's bride from Oklahoma arrived first, was met at the Kimball depot, whisked off to the justice of the peace, taken to the Kimball House for dinner and an overnight stay, and brought out to the homestead the following day. Almost a month later, Caleb repeated the procedure when his bride arrived from Tennessee.

When I stopped by the second time, a complete transformation had taken place around their property. I was surprised to see the uncluttered yard, a white picket fence surrounding "the cottage," and flowered curtains at the windows. Caleb appeared immediately wearing a clean workshirt, patched but freshly laundered bib overalls, and a clean cap. His hair no longer dangled over his eyes, for he had been given a short haircut, probably under a bowl; and white skin around the back contrasted to the rest of his deeply tanned neck. While he worked, the new Mrs. Cummings came out, introduced herself, and gave me a hearty handshake. A small woman some years older than Caleb, she was spry and a great talker with an interesting hillbilly accent. As he finished and I asked the cost of the job, Mrs. Cummings promptly said, "Two dollars." Caleb seemed proud and pleased.

Breaking prairie was an untried experience for me. The plow was excellent and served its purpose well, but the job was far more difficult than I had imagined. I kept working, setting the plow shallow, the sharp upright colter near the front knifing through the turf to form a clean cut as a seemingly endless ribbon of sod turned over the shiny moldboard. I was determined to accomplish what I had set out to do, although the first days caused me to wonder if I had not bitten off more than I could chew.

I knew admitting defeat was impossible for I would surely never hear the end of Pa's "I told you so! What if I had put out the money for a brand new breaking plow, as you'd have had me do!" On and on I went, day after day, fully appreciating what the early pioneers went through and understanding why only the hardy ones endured to face the further anguishes of the prairie. After I could see my goal was not beyond reach, I enjoyed the pleasurable discoveries that awaited me behind rocks and in tall grass. As I bypassed a jumbled pile of large rocks, I found it was a coyote's den in front of which lay bones, rabbit fur, and bird feathers. Some of my discoveries carried an element of danger, for one day I killed a large rattlesnake that blended in color with the nearby rocks. Having heard that where there is one, there are others, I was extremely wary but found no more. In a low place which still held water from the melted snow and spring rains, grass grew green around the water's edge; it was a favorite spot for birds. A shitepoke waded about searching for frogs, and I was careful not to rouse this ragged-appearing heron. Killdeer, protesting my presence at first, ran about in short quick runs and flights screaming warnings to a pair of mallards while their fluffy ducklings bobbed up and down on little waves.

Eventually the long days of plowing came to an end, and we put in flax because we were told it was the best crop in a newly broken field. The rest of this venture had to be left to the grace of God and the whims of nature. I felt a great sense of accomplishment and surprisingly realized I would miss the quiet solitude I had first abhorred. I remembered only the pleasant aspects: my lunches alone in the shade under the wagon, quiet naps while the horses ate their grain, songs of the birds, insect calls, the smell of clean moist earth, fragrant breezes scented by prairie wild flowers, and the colorful evening sunset that let me know it was time to start home to a satisfying meal and a good night's sleep.

WORKING AT BALSTERS

THE PROBLEM of what I would do after the flax was planted was solved by an offer from the Balsters. Alone in the field one day, I was surprised to see Nora and Alberta approaching, because they were not dressed to go anywhere special and obviously were coming to see me. I was sure it had to be more than just a friendly visit.

"Would you," Nora began, "be willing to take care of our farm while our folks are away on a trip? They'll be gone four weeks, and they're willing to wait until you've finished your plowing and seeding." They knew the planting season would soon be over.

The offer was so totally unexpected and her words came so fast I was almost speechless. The girls probably thought I was hesitating about accepting, for Nora added, "Mr. Saunders recommended you."

Mr. Saunders! That really startled me. Did he tell them he had fired me, I wondered. I was afraid to ask.

At home that evening, we discussed the job. Pa thought it was fine, though he could hardly believe it. Of the six Balster children, only two were boys; the older one had taken a job with the railroad the past winter and was a fireman working out of Chadron, Nebraska, and the younger boy was only seven.

"With that bunch of girls," Ma teased, "I bet a lot of work will be going on over there!"

Mr. Balster told me it was their first trip since their marriage. He gave few instructions before leaving: "The girls will do their usual chores. You look after the livestock and plow firebreak around the buildings, haystacks, and the perimeter of the farm. On your way in each noon and night, bring a load of hay." It didn't sound like much until I got started and discovered there would be miles of that firebreak, six feet wide.

The four girls, from nineteen-year-old Nora to eleven-year-old Frieda, were not only neat and pretty, but diligent workers. Nora, "boss of the house," cleaned, made the beds, took care of the laundry, and did most of the cooking. The others fed the chickens, gathered eggs, milked the cows, separated the cream, churned butter, gave skimmed milk to the pigs and calves, drove to Kimball with eggs and butter, did the shopping, took piano lessons, and accomplished a myriad of other things.

I would have been flattered had I thought their neatness of dress, the excellence of our meals, and their general conduct were enhanced because of my presence; I accepted everything as being their normal routine.

Our few moments together, especially at meals, were filled with gaiety, but there was no dallying for work was always waiting. Immediately after the evening chores, the girls took turns playing the piano while we sang all the latest songs, usually for about a half-hour. Following the songfest, the girls lighted their lamps and went upstairs to bed, with their alarm clocks set to go off before daybreak. I found it a very enjoyable four weeks, and the time went by quickly.

I went home each Sunday after chores except one. The younger girls suggested we go fishing that day and have a picnic. They all helped to fry chicken, make German potato salad, bake biscuits, and fill in the corners of the picnic basket with jellies and pickles from their well-stocked cellar.

In a rickety spring wagon, we bumped over a little-used road to a spot on Smith Creek where there were trees and a pond of clear cool water surrounded by overhanging grass. The pond had been formed by a rocky ford, long since in disuse, over which the outflow from the pond gurgled, splashed, and slid on its way.

Eager to get our fishlines into the water, we baited our hooks with dough balls. Almost immediately the gaily painted bobbers were out as far as we could throw them. We didn't care about our mediocre success because we had the picnic lunch and the delightful shady spot to enjoy it. Some black Angus calves came to watch but soon turned away and began to graze.

Tiring of fishing, Nora and I left to look for wild flowers along the creek bank and in the meadow. Most of the flowers were unfamiliar to me. "This is a partridge pea," she pointed out. "These are rattle boxes, and there, some rabbitsfoot clover." We came across low growing purple milkwort and the tall compass plants which have flowers three inches across that always point toward the north. A flash of lightning and a roll of thunder alerted us to a dark cloud overhead. Huge warm raindrops splashed us, but we did not run for cover.

"It will soon be over," Nora said, turning her face toward the sky, arms outstretched. "How I love the rain!"

So different, I thought, from my days in the city, with our oft-quoted Robert Louis Stevenson verse: "Rain, rain, go away, Come again another day." Before we got back to where her sisters had found shelter, Nora's hair was wet and her dress clung to her slender body. With the returning bright sunlight and warm air, glistening raindrops quickly disappeared.

The lovely Sunday outing was spoiled only by those moments when I thought of the decision I would be forced to make the following day. I had been worried since the day I arrived about a young horse that limped slowly around the pasture.

"Blackie," Nora had told me, "was kicked by another horse and has a festered sore on his leg."

My investigation, however, revealed he had a cut tendon, most likely from barbed wire. Cattle stand when caught in wire, but horses struggle until completely exhausted; we usually carried wire cutters for such emergencies. The usual results were ugly scars reducing a horse's value, or cut tendons rendering a horse lame and useless causing him to have to be destroyed. Blackie's wound had become infected, with gangrene setting in so badly it was just a mass of proud flesh seeping yellow pus. Whether it would heal was questionable, and each day it was apparently worse.

Mr. Balster had left no instructions regarding the horse, and I dreaded the thought of destroying him. By Saturday he could no longer reach water, so that day, and again on Sunday, I took him water in a pail.

Early Monday morning I left the house with a gun. Nora saw me, and her face blanched. Frieda, the youngest, shrieked, "Daddy won't want you to!"

Blackie, balanced on three legs, nickered as I approached, his eyes full of hope and trust. He was the first horse I had to shoot, a task I had hoped would never befall me, for I thought horses, next to people were the best things God created.

The rest of the day and part of the night I thought about Blackie. At least I could preserve his beautiful black, silky hide.

While I was skinning the carcass, cattle coming to the water hole must have caught the smell of blood. I heard them first, then saw them, stampeding toward me. My mount, grazing not far away, pointed his ears. Since we were new to each other, I felt fortunate that he stood until I could get hold of the reins, for I never liked being surrounded by excited steers.

I again met with difficulty when I came in the spring wagon to get the hide. The horses would not go near, and the hide was too heavy to carry. I finally managed to back them to it, taking advantage of the wind direction to blow the scent away.

"You made the only decision possible," Mr. Balster told me upon their return, quickly dissipating my concern. "You really needn't have skinned him, but I'm grateful you did," he added. Mr. Balster undoubtedly realized that skinning had been heavy work and turning the horse must have been difficult.

I felt sad about it until the next winter when I saw Blackie's silky coat draped across their laps in the sleigh. Mrs. Balster had backed and trimmed it with black felt, and it was a robe that would be serviceable for many years.

My only misfortune during the stay had been the loss of my wonderful gauntlet gloves that Pa had berated as a foolish luxury. They were somewhere in the big haystack where they had been rolled up in a sling load of hay. As I left, I considerd my four-week stay all too brief, for the general surroundings and the company of the young ladies were far more desirable than being around men in a bunkhouse or working with a threshing crew.

FULL-SCALE FARMING

W HILE I had been working on my special projects breaking prairie, seeding the flax, and working at Balsters, Nick had been far from idle. He had disked last year's cornfield and drilled a new kind of wheat into it.

Bluestem does well in Minnesota where there is enough rainfall, he had learned, but sea-island, a smaller bearded grain, is safer, more drought resistant, and more impervious to rust and smut.

Nick scoffed at the poor equipment, my secondhand plow, and the outworn "old country methods" many of the foreigners had brought with them. Wanting to use modern, improved systems, he courageously approached Pa.

Pa still favored doing everything on a small scale and thought it all too much of a gamble on the vagaries of nature, but he grudgingly went along with Nick. He put himself into further debt with a new Fuller Johnson sixteen-inch sulky plow with four horse eveners, convinced by Nick's insistent, "It will turn over twice as much ground as the old two-horse walker." A new Van Brunt drill replaced inefficient broadcasting; as a result, the wheat was sown evenly, each kernel at the same depth, and every inch of ground utilized, with no loss to roving flocks of cowbirds.

Yellow dent corn, a greater risk than Indian corn, was to be planted in the fields where wheat had grown the previous year.

"Lucky we had some good spring rains this year," Nick told me, as Ed and I looked over the field with him. "The field was blown bare all winter, and I was afraid it would be too dry to sprout the corn. Pa took it upon himself to burn the wheat stubble last fall." The stubble, as I had learned this past winter, holds the snow which saturates the ground to considerable depth when it melts in spring. Everyone, therefore, waits until spring to burn stubble.

Ed started to laugh. "You should have been here that day! Pa set the prairie afire! He was the funniest sight you'll ever see—coming across the field, faster than he ever moved before, and excited: his face was red; he was covered with soot and ashes and hollering that we should do something and get help."

"But don't ever let him know we told you about it," Nick put in. "We thought the whole country might go."

"Yeah," Ed continued, "all that black smoke, flames shooting up, headed for the Burian place. They saw it and were over here right away, Frank and Antone on horseback, and Joe with barrels of water, gunny sacks, and everything else they needed in their wagon. The boys attached a wire to a timber, fastened it to their saddle pommels, and rode, dragging it between them along the sides of the fire. We used the water-soaked sacks to beat out the small flames behind the drag. Those boys were really good—they narrowed that fire down so they had it licked before it reached the firebreak. No one's ever said anything since, but I bet the whole country knows about it."

"Where was Pa?" I asked. "Did he help?"

"Oh, no," Ed exclaimed, "he stayed in the house! He sure looked funny, standing there, watching from the window."

"Say, that reminds me, I haven't seen any of the Burians since I've been home."

"No, and you won't!" Ed announced. "They aren't speaking anymore. Can you blame them? First we caused their dam to go out, and this time we almost burned them out."

Though Ed laughed at Pa's actions, we all knew the fire itself was no joke and fully realized the disaster it could have caused.

Nick was ready to plant the corn. He used the new "check-row" system, stretching a half-mile wire with equidistant lugs the length of the field. The lugs tripped a small lever, making an opening for three kernels of corn to drop. The wire was moved over for every round. With this method, Nick's hills of corn were in straight rows up, down, across, or at any angle; they could be cultivated and weeded in any direction.

Most farmers in the area followed a more haphazard method as they planted their corn in two-row drills. When too many kernels dropped from the hoppers, the corn had to be thinned; when too few, hand planting made up the difference. A rod extending from the side of the planter marked a line the horses were to straddle during the planting of the next two rows. As well-trained as the horses were, some farmers had crooked rows. Tongue in cheek, they explained, "There's more corn in crooked rows." Nick's weedless field and straight corn rows were the talk of the countryside.

Nick plowed deep and his field held the rain. Some of the farmers, to conserve sparse rainfall, bought listers, a double-moldboard plow that formed a ditch or deep furrow at the same time it planted the grain. They had to abandon this remedy when they found that water draining from the higher portions of the furrow drowned the corn in the lower parts. Spelt, a Russian grain claimed to withstand drought, was tried. It grew well but produced little grain; it also brought the Russian thistle, or tumble-weed, that blocked the fences which were later broken down by the wind.

Agnes, in the meantime, had been given an assignment all her own. As millions of tiny green blades pushed their way up on the south slopes in early spring, farmers turned their herds away from the feed racks and out onto the prairies. Commonly seen with each herd was a child, usually a little girl, astride a gentle horse that was too old for more arduous farmwork, and accompanied by a dog. The child's duty was to keep the herd together and out of the grainfield. This became Agnes's job, and she, like the other little girls, found the days long and lonesome.

Pa had warned her: "Woe behold you if you let them get into the grainfield!" At first, Agnes didn't mind the few hours after school in early spring, but the increased hours throughout the spring and summer became annoying. She could look toward the schoolhouse, which stood empty all summer, and envision the clean, neat room that would welcome the little group of students in late fall. She must have dreamed of the social life that awaited her. Last winter she and Ed had taught the other children many games new to them: bean bag, run sheep run, a tisket–a tasket, and London Bridge is falling down. For most of the pupils, school was serious business and the lessons were hard to master, particularly if English was not spoken in their home. Long hours of helping in fields and herding cows had not allowed much time for play and games; most tumbled onto their corn husk mattresses as soon as the milking was over and the cows and horses bedded down.

Eating her lunches alone in the field, Agnes looked forward to the noon gatherings at school when the children opened their tin pails and made exchanges: a piece of jelly bread for a hard-boiled egg, or a slice of German coffee cake for a Bohemian ko-lache. Since there was always a new teacher, Agnes wondered whether she would be greeted by a cross old maid or a lively, happy one like Miss Budlong. Whatever occurred, it would be a big adventure and a welcome change from herding.

Agnes played her harmonica and sang little songs to help pass the time. Bored and alone, she loped in on any little excuse, usually to get an apple, and was sent off again immediately. She complained bitterly of being lonesome and of having to endure the heat. Bothered further by a rash, she said the saddle was hot. Ma told her not to stay on the horse but to dismount and sit on a blanket for relief. Agnes immediately found this was no solution, for she was no sooner seated than the cattle headed for wheat and corn fields. Besides, it was dangerous because there were rattlesnakes in the area.

One day Agnes rode in crying, saying she had seen a big snake. To prove there was nothing to fear, I rode out with her. She held my hand tightly as we walked around kicking at sparse bunches of alkali grass in a low place where the cracked gray earth indicated there had once been a pond. Suddenly Agnes screamed in horror.

"There!" she shrieked. "There!" pointing.

Not more than a short step away, almost at my feet, was a coiled mass of snake of incredible size. My first thought was *Rattler!* even though I had heard nothing. I knew you can never be sure; they have been known to strike without warning. Knowing it had been observed, the snake opened a mouth big enough to engulf a large gopher. It began to hiss, its forked black tongue flicking.

Stunned and angered, I looked about for some object so I could kill it. The snake began to uncoil ever so slowly, its beady eyes fixed on me, its tongue continuing to flick. I could see bulges from gophers or perhaps young rabbits it had swallowed, helping to account for its massive size. It crawled away into tall grass, out of sight. I looked for it for several days afterwards but without success.

Agnes was permitted to change her range to the other side of the farm, but she could not dismiss her fears for a long time. It shook me, too, whenever I thought of it during the next few days. Even though a bull snake is nonpoisonous, a bite can be painful and may become infected. Bull snakes will bite when cornered or, as this one, too gorged to move quickly away from impending danger. Ed's dog Prince had suffered a festering wound from what we had reason to believe was the result of a snakebite.

Pa promised Agnes that after a few good years we would pay off the mortgage on the farm, pay all of our debts, and fence the land so she would not be required to herd anymore. These prospects, always a long way off, seemed even more remote to Agnes when the breezes carried the sounds of talk and laughter from harvest and threshing crews to this seemingly deserted little girl on the lonesome prairie.

HARVEST TIME

B Y THE END OF JUNE, chest-high wheat was turning from a rich green to gold. Well-filled heads of the new wheat waved and nodded in the wind; in more lush places it was so heavy it fell of its own weight. Nick began to talk of buying a binder, and Pa did not protest.

Last year's crop, sparse and low growing, had been harvested by a process known as heading. The header, pushed along by six horses, cut a wide swath; and the heads of grain, elevated in special wagons low on one side and high on the other, were stacked at once. The disadvantage in this method is that stacked grain has to be very dry to prevent heating and mildewing, and when it is dry many kernels fall to the ground in the handling process. Cutting can be done only when the air is dry and there is no dew.

When Nick brought the binder out from Kimball, still crated, Pa shook his head. "Who is going to put it together?" he asked.

Nick, too, may well have had some misgivings. The entire family gathered around and began examining the giant puzzle. There were so many parts; large ones were in their own boxes and smaller ones in cotton bags, all named and numbered.

The bigger parts were assembled quite readily, with Nick directing: "This wheel goes here, that one there, then the windlass that turns and bends the grain into the cutter." Next was the cutter bar and something called a pitman, the purpose of which was to push and pull the cutting sickle. There was a box to hold the twine, arms and fingers to hold the bundle and tie the knots, a platform for finished bundles, a lever to trip and eject them into windrows, various lengths of canvas conveyors, a perforated iron seat, several levers to adjust the cutting height, and another to pull the cutter bar over a rock or other obstruction.

After the binder was assembled, there were many minor

adjustments to make. The bundles had to be tightly packed, but not too tight or so loose they would fall apart, tension on the twine had to be just right so it would not become tangled or break, and knots had to be tied tightly.

Soon the binder stood ready to go. It was a beauty, glossy red and yellow, shining in the sunlight and smelling of fresh enamel. Pa, coming out to look it over, smiled with satisfaction. What is even more important, it worked—almost from the start! The twine broke once or twice and was adjusted; that was all.

I followed behind the binder, placing the bundles into shocks for further drying and protection against the rain. After a few weeks we could thresh direct from the shock, should a thresher come to the neighborhood. Otherwise, for protection from the weather, the grain would have to be placed in stacks, heads inward, butts outward, bundles slanting slightly downward to shed the rain and dew.

Learning we would not have to stack was good news! Aaron Havlik, about two miles away and one of our nearest neighbors, had a threshing machine and wanted to give it a test run not too far from home. Pa made the necessary arrangements. One day the big black engine, pulling the yellow separator, arrived, belching smoke, squealing and groaning, shedding accumulated rust and dust after standing out all winter. Aaron wasn't the kind to keep machinery, regardless of its value, under cover.

"Where do you want the straw stack?" he shouted to Pa over the din.

Pa indicated a spot a good distance from the barn.

Charley, Aaron's oldest boy who at a young age had married a little French girl and wasn't home very much, arrived to act as engineer. Jimmy hauled water for the engine. The three Havliks busied themselves getting things ready, filling oil cups, unrolling and applying a sticky dressing to the twenty-five-foot leather belt, and making last minute adjustments and minor repairs.

A college-type young man, representing the Avery factory, had driven out to help and, if possible, promote sales. "Aaron," he said, looking on, "is the only one who ever makes money. I can never sell him any parts; his outfit holds together with binder twine and barbed wire." It was a fair assertion, but Aaron was also ingenious.

After a few false starts and sudden stops, squealing and wheezing, the belt took hold and wheels began to spin. Soon bundles of grain were being swallowed as fast as we could pitch them. Wicked-looking knives whirled, reaching out to cut the twine. Beaters took over and flailed the grain. With a great turbulence in the bowels of the big yellow machine, a blower whirred, and clouds of straw and chaff were emitted from a large pipe; the wind caught it and tossed it far beyond. The Avery man held his hand in front of the blower for evidence of wheat grains in the straw. He checked the wheat cascading into a wagon for weed seeds and chaff.

"I don't know how Aaron does it," he said satisfied, shaking his head, "but, of course, the Avery Yellow Fellow is a good machine."

Threshing, especially when the harvest had been good, was a time of cheer and good fellowship, even exceeding that of the holidays. Neighbor helped neighbor; wives and daughters brought pies, cakes, and their most tasty dishes. The women arrived early, dressed neatly, with their hair done up as for a party. Mountains of good food included fried chicken, chicken stew with dumplings, red ripe tomatoes, cucumbers, corn on the cob, turnips, carrots, and potatoes with rich cream gravy. The ladies seemed to compete with each other for flattering comments from the men, among whom there was much good-natured bantering.

I felt fortunate to be asked by Mr. Havlik to join his crew from the time we finished our place. It would be a long run, and the pay was good. Before the season was over, I had hauled water, helped pull out the water tank mired along the creek, stoked the engine, hauled coal, and helped make repairs. When all was going well with the threshing rig, I put in my time pitching bundles or shoveling grain. It was back-breaking, muscle-aching work under a relentless sun. Anyone not physically fit could not survive through the day.

When supper was over, we sought the comfort of the straw pile, sometimes falling asleep without shedding our clothes and unmindful of the mosquitoes that sought to pester us throughout the night.

After finishing at the Kovandas, we moved on to the Pitseks, the Burians, the Chapskys, the Urbans, and a dozen more. West of Vega, the names were Mortenson, Nelson, Thorsen, and Ohlsen. Homes and barns bore fresh paint and everything seemed more orderly, but the people lacked the conviviality we found among the Bohemians.

The Lasse Ohlsens had a daughter Kristin, a cute little trick

Universitas
BIBLIOTHECA

of about sixteen, flaxen-haired, with a creamy complexion. Her laced bodice accentuated her short stature and ample hips. As she skipped around waiting on our table, we exchanged glances and smiles. The extra piece of pie she placed before me carried its message well. I met her at the windmill pump where I was almost certain she would come for water to do the dishes.

"Vait," she said, as I helped her with the pail. "Ve pretty soon finish."

The neighbors had gone home for the night, our crew was long since at rest, and the lights in the house were out when she came running breathlessly toward me. We joined hands as she led me to a seat from an old spring wagon in a dark corner by the house. A round harvest moon was rising over a nearby field of ripening corn, and leaves rustled in the soft breeze. The stars hung low and sharp.

For a while we just sat and listened to the cry of an owl and the strumming of cicadas. A pleasant smell came from small leafy plants growing at the side of the house. Kristin pinched a leaf off one and then another, holding them for me to smell.

"Tansy," she explained. "Ve haff it in Sveden. This ve call olt man, this vun olt lady. Vas you born here?"

"No, in Omaha," I answered.

"Omaha?" she repeated. "It's a big city like New York." She remembered New York for its tall buildings. Fearing they might fall on her, she had cried and wanted to walk in the middle of the street. She thought it funny now, "but I never vish to go there again."

We held hands, palms together, our fingers interlaced.

"It's getting chilly," I said, pulling her gently toward me. She nestled closely in the crook of my arm. Her hair against my cheek was soft and smelled clean, of tar soap. She had put on a freshly ironed gingham dress. I was glad I had taken time for a good wash at the water tank. My hair had grown too long, but I had wet it and combed it back. I had shaved for the first time in over a week and put on a clean shirt, something members of our crew seldom did. As Aaron sometimes said, "We may be dirty, but it's clean dirt."

Kristin and I had been sitting there so long I expected her mother or father might call her at any minute. In case they did, I wanted her to know that I surely hoped I would see her again.

"I don't haff a feller," she answered. "Papa don't vant for me to go vith boys."

Her lips were so close I scarcely brushed them with mine as she turned away, changing the mood with "I can hear your watch 'tickling.'"

I could hear it, too, though I tried not to. It was long past bedtime. Her springer spaniel that I had scarcely noticed before must have thought so, too, as he arose at that moment to yawn and stretch his legs.

Rising, I held her close and pressed a kiss on responsive lips.

"I haff neffer kiss a boy before," she said, letting me know it was something special. She sighed and pinched my arms with her small but sturdy hands while groping for words: "It's like—ven the first time—you taste ice cream."

What was there to say? "Let's have more ice cream."

It was near midnight when I lay on my blanket in the straw pile, gazing up at the stars and feeling sort of smug toward the rest of the world.

It seemed as though I had been asleep only a few minutes when I heard the clatter of Charley cleaning out the ashes and preparing to stoke up the engine. The neighbors always had breakfast at home before arriving. Our crew ate at daybreak, feasting on eggs, ham, bacon, fried potatoes, muskmelon, fresh turnips, tomatoes, carrots, and finishing leftover pie and cake from the evening before. Kristin was not around, no doubt still asleep.

This was to be our last day at Ohlsens. We noted a slight breeze, a portent of rain, and by noon, clouds passing over spilled huge drops. Scattered bundles of grain and a number that had broken lay about on the ground. We sat, resting and waiting, until the rain stopped and the sun appeared. Unthreshed grain steamed as it began to dry.

Someone suggested a stick pull, a two-man tug of war in which the contestants, seated on the ground, facing each other, feet together, grasp a stick between them and try to pull each other up. As one after another was eliminated, it became my turn to select an adversary.

Short, stocky Mr. Ohlsen reminded me so much of Kristin and the pleasures of the evening before, I was drawn toward choosing him. To lose to him would be no disgrace, and I felt that I could give a tussle or possibly even beat him. He had not spoken to me all morning. Seeming surprised I should select him, he gave a derisive chuckle.

Once we were seated face to face, he spoke low with a guttural Swedish accent: "Anyone who sits up half the night can't pull anyone."

So he knew our secret! I was glad no one heard him, for if the men had, they might have known to what he referred.

I grasped the pitchfork handle between us with a new determination. He took his hold slowly with an easy confidence and began the pull, easy at first and then harder. His face became crimson as I held. It wasn't going to be as easy as he had expected. His neighbors and the crew looked on with ever greater interest as we tugged and strained, he for his honor, I with a feeling of vengefulness.

Draws are unusual in this game, but that is what it promised to be. My arms ached as though being pulled from their sockets. I was on the verge of giving up when I noticed daylight under him; then it disappeared, but it was a good sign. Since there was hope, I struggled even harder than before, if indeed that was possible. He held his seat, but his hands began to come over to my side of our shoe tops, and I knew he had weakened. With a final tug I pulled him off balance, and knew it was over. I could have pulled him over my head, and he knew it. I let him down gently. He sat resting as I rose and gave him my hand.

"Anyone who can do that can sit up with my daughter anytime," he said, puffing.

The wheat had dried by the heat of the sun aided by the warm breeze, and wheels turned once more. Moments later we were moving on to Thorsens where dinner was waiting.

Though I never saw Kristin again, I thought of her and wondered if she retained her love for "ice cream."

PLEASURES AND DISAPPOINTMENTS

UNHAPPILY, Thorsen's was our final threshing job of the season. We knew it was the last on Aaron's schedule, but the crew felt he would most likely line up one or two more places. I hoped he would; I preferred to move on to at least one more paying job before going home.

The second day at Thorsens I heard a rumor, "Beine's wheat is heating." That meant it would mildew and be unfit even for chicken feed! How could that be, I wondered. Aaron had thought it dry enough for threshing, but judging from the way he did things sometimes there could be some doubt. Sunday I borrowed a horse from Mr. Thorsen and rode home, thinking how sad it was to escape all such disasters as drought, hail, rust, smut, fungus, and grasshoppers, to have such a rare good growing year, and then to realize so little for our efforts. My thoughts focused on Nick and how unhappy he must be. Riding in, I found him working around the barn and was surprised his greeting was so cheerful.

"What's with the wheat?" I asked.

"What do you mean, what's with the wheat?" he replied, puzzled. "Nothing's with the wheat."

Hearing the rumor, he dismissed it at once: "Nothing to it—probably wishful thinking by the Burian boys. We have the wheat stored in the bedrooms. From the road they can see the open windows and no doubt spread the rumor."

I returned to Thorsens that evening with a light heart but with a nettled feeling toward the Burians!

As the week went on, Aaron's wire and binder twine repairs, as ingenious as they were, could no longer hold his rig together. He finally had to shut down, pending the arrival of new parts from the factory. Disappointed, I returned home.

I could always find work to do at our place; it seemed as though it surrounded us. Nick had long since laid by the corn, the final cultivation when the plows are set to throw the soil over exposed roots. Corn never looked lovelier, with row upon row of tassels bending with the wind in military precision and broad, dark green leaves overlapping across the rows. Ears, topped with corn silk, were plump, "in the milk," sugar sweet, and a temptation for the cattle. Once they got a taste of it, they went berserk and it took our combined effort to drive them out. Agnes had to be especially alert, for they would head back again and again.

The Burian cattle caused trouble in our fields, too. Pa, rushing up as fast as his legs could carry him, shook his fist and shouted from a distance: "Get those beasts out of there, and lo and behold you if you ever let that happen again!" His warning was both a threat and a curse, unrivaled anywhere.

Prince often helped to drive out the cows but exacted his

pay by bringing home an ear of corn for himself. Several times each day we saw him going up the road to the cornfield where, finding an ear within his reach, he pulled until he finally tore it loose. Returning triumphant, with frequent stops to rest, he dragged it along. No doubt he enjoyed the sport as much as the corn, for we found partially devoured ears all over the place.

In the flax field the crop, a symphony in tan and brown, was ready for cutting. Thousands of slender branches, terminated by small round pods filled with seeds, rattled with the slightest movement. Because it was a new field, we had to be ever-alert for rattlesnakes. Had there been one, the rattle of seed pods would have made it difficult to hear a warning. We found flax difficult to work into a stack, because branches interlocked and had to be pulled apart.

Sundays provided a welcome break in our work routine, for we were invited to play with the baseball team in Pukwana. There, to my surprise, Big Sobek was the umpire. Nick had learned Big was good on the bases and better on balls and strikes. This news was particularly gratifying because a few previous umpires had difficulty judging Nick's sweeping curve that caught the corners of the plate at an angle. We found Big's decisions to be fair, but whether fair or not, his voice and manner of delivery left little room for doubt or argument; he was nobody's friend.

About the time our work in the fields was finished, new mail-order catalogs arrived from Sears, Roebuck and from Montgomery Ward. The old ones had long since been relegated to the outhouse where they served a useful purpose and where, except for days when it was too cold to tarry, one could thumb through the pages in a manner of window shopping. With the crops in and being marketed, the catalogs arrived at a favorable time. There had been so many months of doing without; there were so many needs and an even greater number of wants, it was difficult to know where necessities left off and luxuries began.

We made up long lists from which a number of items were subsequently eliminated or for which cheaper ones were substituted. In addition to a Sharpless cream separator, harness, horse collars, and a farm wagon, there were work clothes for all, good suits for Nick and me, school clothes for Ed and Agnes ("extra large for growing children"), yard goods, a barrel churn, and kitchen things for Ma. For Pa there was an easy chair; he had complained that the kitchen chairs were uncomfortable for one of his "heft." A pipe and a canister of tobacco were listed as a substitute for cigars which Pa, with an assist from Ma, had finally concluded were too expensive.

The pictures and descriptions in the catalogs excited our imaginations. We could hardly wait for the order to arrive. When it finally did, the huge packing boxes were opened with the entire family looking on in eager anticipation. There was some elation, considerable disappointment. Some items were reported out of stock, others proved to be inadequate for what we had intended, and some clothing did not fit properly.

Ed's suit with his first long pants turned out to be a coarse gaudy check that, had it fit, would have given him the appearance of a carnival barker. The trousers came up to his armpits. Nick said, "Looks like Ed got a vest along with his pants. If they're not hiked up, that seat will hold a bushel of potatoes."

Pa couldn't get used to his new pipe and found that the easy chair wasn't so "easy" or comfortable as he had expected.

With our anticipation far exceeding the realization, our first mail-order experience was not particularly happy. For some reason, however, not a single item was returned for adjustment. One of the more satisfactory purchases was the new farm wagon, a Cooper running gear in brilliant red, with a shining, dark green Deer and Weber box with yellow trim. We could still use our old wagon too, lined in places with sacks to prevent the grain from spilling through.

Pa hadn't driven a team to Kimball since shortly after we arrived, but now he couldn't resist taking the first load of wheat to town in the new wagon and insisted that Ma go along. "You just have to get off the place," he said. It was a momentous occasion for both. Ma had not been to Kimball since our initial stay at the Kimball House.

We loaded the wheat, hitched our best team, and assisted Ma up onto the spring seat. She again looked every bit the lady in the pretty city clothes she had worn upon our arrival: the long full skirt of charcoal gray, the off-the-face hat with its bird wings, the polished high-buttoned shoes, and her hair pompadour over a rat. All that was missing was the shirred pink taffeta shirtwaist with the high collar. It had gone so well with her charcoal gray suit, but when she went to get it from her trunk she found it had disintegrated at every fold. Looking at her all too few precious possessions, she recalled the words of the woman at the junction in Minnesota: "When I came here, I looked like you." Had the words not implied that when going back Ma might look like her?

Pa sat beside her looking like an aristocrat or city salesman, wearing his tailored suit, a black Homburg hat, and gloves. His freshly lit cigar perfumed the summer air as it had each morning in Omaha.

"Shimmel!" he shouted to the horses as he slapped their rumps. It was the term he had always used whenever he started out in good spirits; what significance it had or what it meant I never knew.

I sat on the kitchen stoop watching the wagon bump along over the prairie, disappearing for a while beyond a rise, appearing again far beyond, until it was out of sight.

I thought of Pa's watch with the heavy gold link chain and the fob dangling from it across his ample belly. My first recollection of the watch was of Pa holding it to our ears and our wondering what caused it to tick. I remembered the esteem he held for it as he showed us the beautifully embossed numerals and the hands which appeared to be filigreed with gold lace. The fob, in the shape of a shield, was backed with iridescent gold stone that I thought must have been a rarity. The face of the fob bore the emblem of Pa's lodge superimposed by the letters "A.O.U.W.," which he mispronounced "A-O-Ju-W."

The lodge, in which he held office in Omaha, had meant much to him. He had taken keen delight in attending the weekly meetings and the monthly smokers. On meeting nights Ma had kept us children up, huddled around her in the kitchen, until long after our usual bedtime, for she had never overcome her fear of the city. She had ears for every sound, however slight, until she heard the click of the gate latch and knew the approaching footsteps were Pa's. Then she hustled us off to bed so he would not know she had kept us up. She held fears, too, for Pa's safety, for his walk home was along lonely streets and through darkened woods.

The trip to Kimball proved to be a tonic for Pa, and for days afterwards he was in a loquacious mood, telling in detail about every little incident both in town and along the way. After the wheat was sold at the elevator, he encouraged and helped Ma with her purchases of store cookies, candy, fresh fruit and meat—

luxuries we so seldom had, especially during summer months. Then Pa "attended to business," calling at the Whitbeck and Lombard Bank where he was treated royally and had a long visit with Mr. Lombard. He paid off the interest on a chattel loan and on the farm and promised that before the year was out he would reduce the mortgage. By way of celebration he spent a pleasant moment or two over a drink at Sobeks, leaving there with a bottle of schnapps and a box of cigars.

Ma had waited without complaint, seated on the wagon, for there was nowhere to go: no hotel lobby, no library, no park, not even a bench beneath a tree, for there were no trees. "We must do this again some day," Pa said to Ma when they arrived home, but he must have known that day was a long way off.

I had hoped to go back to threshing again, but the season, for Aaron, had come to an abrupt close. I learned that his repaired rig had gone through a bridge. No one expressed any surprise, for, as they said of him, "Aaron goes over a bridge first and then goes back to inspect it for safety."

Big Sobek, also threshing, had finished with wheat and converted to flax, which experienced farmers said was difficult to thresh and hard on the machine. Jobs were few and far between. The Burians had a small field across from the schoolhouse, started after and perhaps inspired by mine. From our house we saw Big's machine pull in and almost at once heard its angry whine as it tore into the tough, resisting fibers and woody stems.

In the late afternoon, with a pale sun casting long shadows toward the east, Pa went for a leisurely stroll. Seeing him head south slowly on the schoolhouse road, I decided to take my shotgun and hoped to flush some prairie chickens that frequented our strawstack in search of grain. Attracted by the call of the threshing machine, I walked around that way, approaching from the off side. It would be fun to watch the threshing rig swallowing bundles of grass, blowing out chaff and straw, and to see the stream of slippery flax seeds sliding down, filling the grain wagons. I had already ejected the shells from my gun, but with the sight that greeted me I reloaded hurriedly.

Pa was defenseless as Big was menacing him with a huge monkey wrench. Big's face, close to Pa's, was livid, and he was shouting, "I ought to kill you! I'll knock your brains out!" Trying to avoid him, Pa stepped back. Big continued to crowd him, with teeth bared like a madman, hurling invectives, with the wicked looking weapon held over Pa's skull. "I ought to kill you!" he repeated again and again between curses.

Instinctively I moved my gun into position, my finger on the trigger. When Big saw me through his blinding rage, I was so close to him he was looking into the gun barrel. Taken by surprise, he lost all interest in his quarry. Big had been around guns enough to respect one pointed in his direction. This one was loaded, cocked, and there was a nervous finger on the trigger. As his eyes took in the gun, his face blanched around a stubble of black beard. His heavy jowls sagged.

As we both stood motionless, he started to speak but decided not to. I kept him covered, in suspense, for a long moment before shifting the gun so it wasn't directly on him. Big accepted the gesture as I had intended and moved away slowly. In the intensity of the moment I had scarcely noticed the whine of the machine had ceased and men were standing around watching.

"It will stay there until it rots," said Big, almost inaudibly. I had not the least idea what he meant.

Pa was heading toward home, looking back with almost every step. I walked slowly behind. After ejecting the shells once more, I held them in my hand and gazed at them, trying to make sure in my confused mind they were still intact.

After feeding the stock and bedding them down, I could delay no longer; I entered the house. The family was already seated for supper, but Pa wasn't there. "He had one of his stomach upsets," Ma said, "and doesn't feel well." The rest of the family, not knowing, may have slept well, but I lay awake a good part of that night wondering what Pa had done or said that made Big want to kill him.

I could hardly wait until the Burian flax was threshed and the rig had moved on before going up to where the Burian boys were cleaning up the spillings. Though the rest of the family seemed to have earned their ire, the boys had never indicated any ill feeling toward me, and I had even had several dances with their sister Emma at a recent party.

"Big fully expected to thresh your flax," the older boy said, "and reasonably so, since it is on adjoining land, and there is some doubt as to whether Aaron Havlik would be able to do the job. Everyone thought your Pa had come over to make the necessary arrangements."

Big, in his customary manner, had not greeted Pa and didn't

wait for Pa to say anything about hiring him. "We'll pull in to your place Tuesday," Big had said in his usual brusque tone.

"No," Pa replied, "Aaron does my threshing."

That filled me in on what had happened before my arrival. The older Burian continued: "Well, you saw it. After that, Big went crazy mad—don't know what would have happened if you hadn't shown up. Big said, 'No one is going to thresh your flax,' and I guess that's that. Nothin' you can do about it."

I went back and broke the news to the family as best I could. It made me sick to my stomach; fears of what could have happened to Pa alternated with the prospect of unthreshed and unsold flax. Shortly after, with a fever, I suffered nightmares. In my nightmare the flax stacks were burning; in an inferno of flame and smoke, I could hear Big's jeers and curses as we tried to beat out the fire. I awoke sweaty and shaking. In spite of my fever, I couldn't wait until morning to go up to the field to assure myself the stacks were still there.

The whole neighborhood surely must have learned about our trouble, but they pretty well avoided the subject.

Sy, during one of our now rare meetings, was almost joyful: "I hear you dehorned the big bull." It gave me little or no satisfaction; my mind was more on the loss of the flax. After all, Big had had the last word.

EFFORTS TO RECOVER OUR LOSS

WITH NO ALTERNATIVE, we had to become reconciled to our loss on the flax and work hard to recoup. The corn was ready for picking, and we eagerly went to the field so early each morning we had to wait until it became light enough to distinguish the ears among the dark leaves.

Working late, we made our way home at nightfall. After a hearty supper, usually fat roast duck, we shoveled our loads by lantern light and fell into bed after removing only our shoes and overalls.

Our baseball experience proved helpful, for our hands and wrists were so supple and strong that with the aid of the corn hooks strapped to our palms we could part the husk, grasp the ear, break it off, and toss it into the wagon all in one smooth motion. With overhand, underhand, and side tosses, we rattled ears rhythmically against the sideboards, in noticeable contrast to the awkward motions and irregular thuds in the nearby Burian field.

Working every day including Sundays, we rested only once when forced to by a mighty storm that lasted almost two days. It came upon us suddenly with blinding flashes of lightning and cannonading thunder. Torrents of rain poured from black clouds, rushed along between corn rows, splashed, and gurgled, heaping piles of hailstones at every turn. We took the slam boards down to cover us as we lay atop the corn in the wagon. The horses needed no guidance to make their way over the familiar road from our cornfield to the barnyard and the shelter of the roof over the corncribs and the drive between. After the horses came to a stop the roar of hail continued. With the wind driving it toward us we were pelted whenever we peered out.

Finding the corncribs gone after the storm gave us the strangest feeling. The floors alone remained, and a trail of corn and broken boards stretched across the prairie. Neither our house nor any of our other buildings appeared damaged. In the house, Pa and Ma had heard nothing over the roar of the storm.

The experience gave us an opportunity to swap stories, whereas previously we had only listened. One homesteader told of waking one morning to find his cabin in the pasture, where the wind had set it down after lifting it up and over a fence. He had slept through the move and said, "I'm going to leave it right where it is unless the wind decides to blow it back, of course." A little experience of mine during threshing west of Vega had been impossible to tell because no one believed it: As I had headed for the barn slightly more than half a mile away to seek shelter from a storm, the pitchfork I carried over my shoulder suddenly disappeared. The men in the barn had just snickered: "Now why would you be takin' your pitchfork with you? None of us took ours." The following day I found it standing upright in the field about fifteen steps from the road. "Don't kid us," they laughed. "You put it there. If lightning hit that wet fork, you wouldn't be here to tell about it!"

Our only other experience was relatively minor and had occurred earlier that same year. After some heavy lightning, we had come into the house to find the kitchen in a mess. Stew meat and vegetables were on the ceiling, potatoes in one corner and on a chair, and pots and pans strewn about among soot and ashes. Ma, her face black with soot, was beating out live coals with Pa's hat. "Lightning must have come down the stovepipe," she said. "You should have seen it! Blew everything sky high!" Looking in the mirror, she had to laugh with us, but grimaced, saying, "The bump on my head isn't funny. I must have been hit with a stove lid." Our supper was a bit late that night!

We never rebuilt the corncribs but piled our corn in a heap on the ground until we could haul it to town. I managed to get a few cornhusking jobs at neighboring farms and learned the pay was even better than for threshing. We worked on an incentive scale, so much per bushel, and my long agile fingers earned the biggest paychecks.

When crops are good, prices are usually low; we got only about nine dollars for each corn load three boards high. Nick blew the receipts of one whole load for an old buggy Pa thought we didn't need. The top was gone and the cushions worn through, but after several coats of black and red paint, it looked quite good. Pa still looked at it skeptically and turned to Nick: "I hope you aren't figuring on going with a girl—one of the Bohunk girls?"

Nick looked at the buggy and laughed. "It's good enough to take a wife out riding, but hardly suitable for courting. What self-respecting Bohunk would ever be seen in it!"

Nevertheless, Pa told Ma: "I think it's high time I tell the boys some of the facts of life." In doing so, he thought no one a more fit example than himself. "I never kept company with a girl until I was in a position to marry," he pointed out. "I was thirty then, and that was time enough." We calculated that Ma was only eighteen, but he didn't mention that.

"I never had a top buggy and sporty team of horses," he continued. "Your mother, like any sensible girl, accepted my thrift as a virtue." He recalled with pride he had not spent any money on her. His only gift to her had been a small photograph album after they became engaged. When he came to see her, he brought peppermints which she liked and which happened to be his favorite candy as well. "Choose a girl from a good family," he admonished, concluding his advice. By "good family," we understood his meaning to be "a prosperous one," implying also she should be healthy and strong enough to help with farm work. We remembered hearing that one of our neighbors, frail Mrs. Stille, had to call her husband in from the field to fetch a pail of water.

While Nick, now nineteen, was not serious about any girl and seemed to care little for social contacts, I liked to mingle and took in a few dances. He usually came along but would not have gone himself. The fiddle or accordion music was often poor, the floor rough, and the girls mostly clumsy and rustic. Everyone gave evidence of the lack of bathing facilities and smelled of whatever fuel was used at home: coal, hay, corn-cobs, or cow chips. At other times fellows sometimes got together for card games, usually pitch or high five; or we called at the homes of the girls, where the chief entertainment was perusing the mail-order catalogs. The girls found the underwear section a convenient time to withdraw to the kitchen to make coffee and prepare to serve the refreshments.

There was some mutual admiration between Nick and Bertha Piskule, who was tall, willowy, and athletic. Annie Pitsek, who preferred to be called Annette, also interested him because of her dancing. How she could shake it in a polka and skip about in a square dance! Pa sought to disparage her by referring to her as "Annie Pisek." Nick thought Mary Beranek was the prettiest of all. She would have been a dreamy-eyed beauty if she had only kept her shoes buttoned and hadn't worn her older brother's coat with sleeves dangling over her hands. She swore like a mule skinner while herding cows, and her melodious voice could be heard for a mile. It was fun to watch her run because she invariably lost one or both shoes.

Each fall the new schoolteacher was of interest to all the young men in the area. To court one was a high honor, and to marry one would have been the ultimate. Miss Budlong, the most interesting by far, was still discussed and compared to the others, especially when the new one, old maid Hatch, arrived in Lyon Township. Before long, the children referred to her as "Miss Hatchet" and "Old Miss Hatchetface."

She stayed with the Balsters, as the teachers had for years. It seemed a natural arrangement because their home had extra room and transportation to the school. The Balsters also seemed to enjoy the arrangement and at no time indicated it was less than ideal. We were surprised when Mr. Balster, after two months of the new term, begged us to take Miss Hatch "for a while" and gave a number of reasons why we should. Pa had to agree that the burden of boarding the teacher had always fallen on the Balsters and it probably was time someone relieved them. The twenty-five dollars a month for board, room, and transportation was the final inducement. Pa and Ma agreed there might be some benefit and pleasure derived from having company during the long, cold, dreary winter, and we thought it would be fun, too, although Ed and Agnes didn't seem overly happy about it.

Our enthusiasm quickly dissipated when we found that Miss Hatch was uncommunicative and kept to her room except for meals which she ate in silence. Pa and Ma tried to be hospitable even though the woman's presence disrupted the normal routine of our household. Pa had to be on his best behavior and had to discontinue some all-too-casual habits. Weekends and school holidays were most trying for Pa. "I feel like a visitor in my own home," he complained. "Try to get her out of the house." This was difficult because there was no place for her to go.

Nick and I took her over to Havliks one Saturday night. Admittedly, the place was not orderly, far from it, but not so cluttered as to make Miss Hatch as uncomfortable as she indicated. Mrs. Havlik served bowls of piping hot oyster stew, about the finest delicacy and luxury she could imagine, but Miss Hatch would have none of it, bluntly stating: "I don't like oysters." The large family of little Havliks, a few scarcely tall enough to reach the table, glanced about shyly with dancing eyes and enjoyed every slurp.

Our next effort at sociability was to take the teacher to a dance. We accepted her reluctance as shyness but decided later that she was just plain disagreeable. She refused all offers to dance or to mingle with any groups. Throughout the evening she sat as though bored, showing no interest in the music, refreshments, or people, and waited impatiently for the party to end.

By this time Pa had made it known to us that he disliked her. Furthermore, Ed and Agnes were giving such incredible reports of the school day that I took advantage of a cold blustery day to stay and observe. "The weather's too bad for Nick and me to work outdoors," I told Miss Hatch upon our arrival at the schoolhouse. "I might as well stay at school today and save myself the trip home and back." Unknown to Miss Hatch, I had put extra food in Ed and Agnes's lunch pails that morning for my needs and had told Ma my plan.

Everything Ed and Agnes had reported was true. Miss Hatch actually couldn't spell. She greatly resented my lack of diplomacy in attempting to assist her in front of the class. Arithmetic proved less difficult because she had the "teacher's book" with answers to the problems. Along with reading and a little penmanship, these were the only subjects she attempted to teach to her class of eight scholars. The enrollment had dwindled after Miss Budlong's departure. The children had little respect for Miss Hatch.

We gradually discontinued our valiant though futile efforts to please her at home. One Sunday she had a visitor, a well-dressed man who drove up in a livery rig. That she had been expecting him was evident, for she came out dressed in warm clothing and carrying two packed bags.

"I'll get your trunk," he said, starting toward the door, but Pa blocked his way and made a gesture of rubbing his forefinger and thumb together, a symbol which was most familiar to us.

"I didn't bring any money with me," the man said. "I'll send you a check."

"The check won't be necessary," said Pa. "Bring the money when you come for the trunk."

The man reached into his pocket for his purse, looked inside, and, surprised, found two ten-dollar bills and a five. Nick allowed him to struggle with the trunk alone until he asked, "Can someone give me a hand?"

When they were gone, Pa placed the money in the deep slash pocket of his pants and smiled as he settled back in his easy chair. He then lighted a cigar, tilted his head back, and blew a huge puff of smoke toward the ceiling. "Boys," he said, "put the base burner back in Mama's and my room. If there is anything I like, it's comfort."

School would be closed for a few weeks until Mr. Balster could sign another teacher to complete the term. No one was particularly concerned because "Balster always finds one some-where!" A few farmers were happy the community could avoid the expense for a while, claiming, "Twenty-five dollars is too much to pay when you can get a good hired hand for that!"

Nick had not allowed the presence of our guest to distract him from a full work schedule. After every snow storm, he trudged up to the flax stacks to clear away the drifts. The rest of us, knowing no one dared dispute Big Sobek, had resigned ourselves to the loss. Nick alone retained a spark of hope that someday the flax would be threshed. Did he possibly think Big would relent? Certain Nick was headed for inevitable disappoint-ment, I wished my nightmare had been true, that the stacks had gone up in flames.

PARTY LINE

WHILE MISS HATCH was boarding with us, Nick began a new project that kept him outdoors from day-light until dark. Previous failures such as the dam, the icehouse, and trees that refused to grow did not discourage him from starting his new venture. "I'm going to put in a tele-phone line," he announced, to our amazement. It was a wild idea the rest of us would never have thought of. Speechless and wide-eyed, we looked at one another until Ma tactfully said, "That's a nice idea, Nick, but don't you think it's too much work?"

Pa said, "I doubt we need it."

Ed wondered, "Would it work?"

In spite of our misgivings, Nick persuaded me to join him. Day after day in all sorts of weather we dug postholes. The ground was sometimes rocky; and wherever it was frozen we thawed it with lukewarm water from the artesian well. Finally the last posthole had been dug. Days, weeks, and months of backbreaking toil came to an end. Nick jubilantly went to town for poles and wire. We set the first load, rough two-by-fours, and strung the wire. The result looked like match sticks held together by a single thread stretching across a rippling sea of unbroken white. On overcast days the sun gave only feeble assurance the wire was there at all.

Although there was no urgency for completion, Nick couldn't stand being idle, especially when the job was so nearly finished. Impatience got the better of him. "I just have to get some poles," he declared one morning as if on impulse. Hastily he threw a load of corn onto the sled and headed for town. "I'll be back early," he promised.

Nick found the going slow across the frozen snow until he reached the main road. Even there travel had been almost non-existent. Nothing short of an emergency usually impelled one to go so far in such weather.

Since Nick had said he would be back early, his return should have been sometime before four-thirty and dusk. By five o'clock it was pitch dark, obliterating all guideposts along the way. Ed looked out the door and remarked, "He'll have to travel by the seat of his pants," a colloquialism he had picked up and preferred using instead of "instinct." Ma waited supper. When Nick had not arrived home by six, we didn't know what to think. Ma served the meal, and we ate in silence, listening. The only sound was the sigh of the wind around the eaves, accompanied by a low whistling as it came up through cracks in the floor and around the windows. Before supper we had placed lamps in all the windows to cast their feeble light in each direction. What little we could do wasn't much.

The minute supper was over Pa and Ed bundled up against the bitter cold and went out with lighted lanterns, Pa north and Ed south to aid in making a bigger target. I saddled Big Ben, our strongest and most dependable horse, and headed in the direction Nick should come. Beyond sight of any light from the lanterns I slowed Ben's pace and stopped to listen. But to listen for what? I scarcely knew what I could expect to hear. To call out or to shout would be to no avail, because Nick's fur-lined cap and high sheepskin coat collar over his ears would prevent him from hearing. Peering into the darkness was useless, for I could barely see the tips of Ben's ears. I knew, too, that Ben's instincts and senses were keener than mine, and he would be certain to neigh at the first sight or sound of Nick's team. Ben's tracks were being covered by the swirling powdery snow almost as soon as they were made.

I recalled how Jupe had lost his way on this very prairie and probably had found it again only because it was a moonlight night and the trail had not been covered with snow. I also remembered a newspaper account of how Charley Gingerly, the driver of the Kimball-Waterbury stage and his passenger, a young schoolteacher, "had suffered twenty-two awful hours before being found only five miles from Kimball." Charley survived but had to have his feet amputated, and Miss Allen died at the Kimball House. Others could tell of experiences only slightly less tragic, and there were many near-misses. These thoughts spurred me on as I turned further to the south where the greater danger lay among small washes widening into deep ravines, sudden drop-offs, and cutbanks near the creek.

I rode on, plunging through one drift, attempting to skirt another, at the same time trying to retain some sense of direction. I carried little hope that my efforts would prove to be of value or that I could be anywhere near my objective in all the vastness. When I reached a point where the draws seemed to be deeper, I cut toward my left. Ben, with natural instinct, weaved in and around, stopping short whenever he sensed danger.

During a lull in the wind, I thought I heard a sound. It was a strange sound that seemed to come from toward the creek. I uncovered my ears and cupped them against the sting of the snow and wind but heard nothing. Knowing it could have been only hope and desire playing on my imagination, I nevertheless rode on toward the sound and its mysterious source. I heard it again: light taps as though metal against metal, seeming to come from afar. Hearing it once more, I thought it sounded more like the tinkle of a bell. I wondered what it could be. There was nothing out that way for miles, and surely it could not be a cowbell or a bell on any other animal, for the animals in the prairie country wore no bells.

Being sure of a sound, though not knowing its cause, I spurred Ben on recklessly, trusting him to keep his footing. Disappointment followed when the tinkling ceased, but I continued to press on shouting "Yippee," the cowboy's call, until it seemed to be only a whisper dissipated by the wind. Then I got a response, and another, and I knew it was Nick.

Suddenly I came upon Nick's team before I knew they were

so close. The back of the sled had slid at a perilous angle into a draw, and Nick was tossing poles over the down side. Saying little, I dismounted and began helping him unload. I tied my saddle rope to the back of the bob, and with a loop around the saddle horn helped to pull the sled out. By then, some of Nick's sense of direction had returned. He knew from the rough terrain that he had veered to the south but said he thought he had by-passed our place and was all for turning back.

"Follow me," I said.

Nick hesitated a moment, still not certain of directions, and then slowly turned his team around. I gave Ben his head to see what he would do. He didn't go due north as I would have done before turning due west. Ben cut across at an angle, which was all right with me; I just hoped he knew what he was doing. When we got into a rough spot, I was certain we were in the old flax field and got down to test for stubble to make sure. I had to slow Ben down when he began taking long strides, blowing steam. He knew he was on familiar ground; he had practically lived on that strip for weeks pulling the plow along each foot of every furrow. Nick's team, dead tired, was scarcely able to keep up but seemed to get their second wind when we passed the flax stacks and they could see the lights of home.

A few days later when the wind was almost still Nick and I went back and found the gully in which the snow-covered poles lay. After the tedious job of pulling each one up with the aid of a rope, Nick looked around. "My God!" he exclaimed, as he understood what his fate might have been. If even one of his horses had lost footing that night, he, the sled with its heavy load, the horses, and all would have rolled down and over protruding rocks into a brush and snow-covered ravine.

Ma often said, "It's fortunate that George decided to make his search toward the south," but I felt the real credit for Nick's rescue should go to a mail-order harness. It was not the good set with leather traces but the cheapest in the book, the one with chain tugs and extra links, that tinkled.

When we got the new poles set and the wire strung, our final task was the installation of the phones, which were considered quite an attractive marvel. In each home, the large wooden case was securely fastened in a prominent place on the living room wall. Nick had invited six other families onto our line, and each had put in the necessary poles and wires to reach from the line to their house. Nick purchased the telephone instruments and dry cell batteries by mail order from Sears, Roebuck.

With the cooperation of the telephone company, to which we were connected at Pukwana, we incorporated as the East Vega Telephone Company. The Swedish settlement had carried the line from Pukwana to Vega. With information Nick obtained from the Swedish families, we had been able to bring the line east from Vega to our place, a distance of over four miles. There were other mutual companies west of Vega, all the way to Pukwana. In our company, as in the others, the original families received life tenure granted by the Articles of Incorporation. The telephone company made no charge for the connection and received remuneration only for long distance calls. We could reach lines west of Vega and Pukwana by calling Fousek's store in Vega where there was a switch. All calls to Pukwana and through Pukwana were long distance, with a toll charged by the telephone company.

Conversations on the first calls were somewhat garbled but were of interest to everyone. Each receiver came off the hook with no attempt to conceal background noises. All were delighted with the telephone and quickly adjusted to hearing: "Who is this? . . . ssst, xx . . . crackle . . . zz. . . . Can you hear me? . . . spt . . . ss . . . pop . . . zzzz . . . I can hear you . . . xxzz! xx . . . sp . . . zoom . . . snap . . . pow . . . Oh, hell, it's that dam' Sara on the line . . . wee . . . shptzz . . . wee-eee . . . Get off the line, Joe. Mary? Mary? Is that you? I kin hardly hear you . . . zz . . . shhh . . . sppp . . . wham! Talk a little louder. Keep quiet, kids . . . xx . . . spt . . . xx . . . Mary, this is important. Frank said to tell you that he . . . xx . . . zz . . . spppt . . . bang!" Then there was silence! To check the lines, Nick called different numbers and if he got no answer, he went out along the line checking grounds, insulators, and wires.

With no rules and no precedents to go by, no one had any basis for criticizing another. We were annoyed at first by our neighbors' habit of listening in, which we thought was as unacceptable as reading another's mail. Soon, however, we too became eavesdroppers, with the exception of Ma, who said, "They're only gassing!" and Pa, who claimed he had better things to do, commenting, "Who wants to listen to that drivel, especially those Beraneks!" The rest of us had some disconcerting moments when the conversations switched from English to Bohemian. "Why do they do that," Ed asked, disgusted, "when they know we're the only ones on the line that can't understand both languages?"

Everyone got used to hearing the Piskules' ring—two longs and a short—because Bertha received more calls than anyone else on the line, and the Pitseks' one long and two shorts, where Annie, answering, "Hello, this is Annette," ran a close second. We enjoyed listening most to Mary Beranek after we found that her phone conversations, like her talk in the fields, were interspersed with cuss words. We decided she had learned them from her older brothers and, no doubt, did not understand the meanings.

Two short rings was a general call; a call at night was always an emergency. Mrs. Havlik, after her experience of fifteen births, was regarded as a competent midwife, and Aaron, her husband, ably performed veterinary duties. Wencel Pitsek could set broken bones, and Mrs. Plos who had learned to use Indian remedies and often swore by them, always had a dripping skunk skin behind her kitchen stove and could furnish skunk grease on a moment's notice. It had served her well as a remedy for pneumonia, pleurisy, or the comon chest cold.

Ma never used the phone, but Pa called Kimball once, and talked so loud Ma chided him: "Why not just stick your head out the window?"

The telephone, enriching our lives and those of the entire rural community, forged an ever-growing kinship among the people on our party line. Favors asked and calls for help always brought a ready response. Everyone began to save money on farm equipment by realizing that arrangements to exchange a mower for a rake, or a plow for a harrow, could be made quickly and easily. "Why," they asked, "should we each have a complete set of tools and equipment that, used for a few weeks each season, stands out to weather and rust?"

For the young, the telephone became a plaything and a diversion; but of more importance, it gave a feeling of security to all. Nick and I were pleased with the result, and the Kimball *Graphic* reported our successful completion of the enterprise, calling it "A milestone—communication with the outside world!"

WILD HORSES

THERE'S NO WORK in winter and no use seeking it. Jobs this time of year are scarce as hen's teeth," Pearly Gates at the Kimball livery stable told me, "but if I hear of anything, I'll sure let you know." He was always willing to turn a favor, like that time he got me to do a favor and take Mrs. Schulty out to her husband's homestead and I froze my feet.

The next time I got to town, sometime in February, I stopped by to see Pearly again.

"Say, you still lookin' for a job?" he asked. "There is a fellow, name of Reber, rounding up wild horses west of the river. Pays well, but I don't suppose you'd want to get mixed up with that. It's rough, real rough!" Pearly shook his head dubiously.

With the telephone line finished, I was getting tired of sticking around home. "I'm ready to take anything," I assured Pearly. "Just tell me where the job is."

Nick drove me over the next day, Sunday. With Pearly's directions—"Follow the section lines. Four miles north, sixteen miles west of Gannvalley, a white house, long red barn surrounded by high corrals made of Indian poles"—we had no trouble finding Reber's place. It stood out by itself on a wind-blown flat, miles from the nearest neighbor.

Reber looked me over and showed us a bunch of horses that he had just corralled. "Think you can handle them? These aren't plow horses," he warned. "There're some mean ones in there."

Nick looked at me doubtfully, but I ignored him. Reber agreed to pay me top hand wages but made it clear, without actually saying so, that he expected top hand work. His offer of thirty-five dollars a month was five dollars more than a ranch foreman's pay. With no experience breaking horses, I accepted, feeling fortunate to earn so much especially at this time of year. Nick got my gear and wished me luck as he left, eager to get home before dark.

Reber took me to the bunk shack and told me to come up to the house as soon as I got settled. The shack smelled of rats, leather oil, and the ever-present Watkins Horse Liniment. Reber wasn't a big man, no taller than my five feet eleven, and a few pounds heavier, about 168, but he looked rugged and moved easily. As he walked away, I thought he was too trim-looking and well-groomed for a man in his job even if it was Sunday, but I guessed the reason when I got to the house and met his wife.

Belle, as he called her, was younger by about ten years. She looked about twenty, maybe twenty-two, and she had most likely led an easy life. She was real pretty in a fragile sort of way with a complexion as pale as pearls.

I was reminded of a book I'd read, *Chip of the Flying U,* in which a city girl went west for her health and found romance with a rugged horse wrangler. Reber even outdid "Chip" as the answer to a maiden's prayer. Besides his good looks, he didn't smoke or drink, and he went to church on Sunday. I told myself no one could be that perfect and decided he was either putting on an act or his reformation took place after he met her. There had to be some explanation.

The house was neat and feminine looking with lace curtains and dainty doilies. Belle, every hair in her pompadour in place, wore a fancy white shirtwaist. Feeling uncomfortable in this atmosphere, I was glad to learn my meals would be served on a little table on the back porch, just off the kitchen.

I had no more than started to work when I learned the reason for Reber's generosity. The work was dangerous—not so much to one's life as to his limbs, hands, and feet. If a wrangler escaped injury over a period of time, it was due to sheer luck! I didn't expect to stay long and decided a person had to have an adventurous spirit to do that work.

Meals were somewhat of a problem. Because of my always-dirty work clothes the clean white tablecloth was a bother, and I put a newspaper over the place where my arms rested. The food, all store bought, was better than any I had ever known, but there was never enough of it for a person doing hard work fifteen hours a day. Reber asked more of me than of himself, like getting me up at five and then going back to bed himself for another hour or two. Mealtime was a bit lonesome since I was the only hand. Nor did Reber offer much companionship otherwise, for he spent much time with Belle, especially when she was ailing, as she often was.

I put in most of my Sundays working because there wasn't anything else to do, but after the Rebers left for church, I always looked around the kitchen for something to eat and then took a nice long nap.

Reber never gave any advice or even helpful suggestions, just orders. "Take the wagon, go down to the dam for a couple barrels of water," the directions for one of my first errands, was a typical example. I unknowingly chose a place where the ice wasn't thick enough to hold. After the barrels were filled the back wheels broke through. I had to scramble for the barrels, find a better spot, and refill them. The next time I went for water, Reber handed me his watch. I understood the implication, but, having no intention of timing myself, put the watch in my jacket pocket without looking at it. At the dam the watch slipped from my pocket, hit the ice, skidded, and disappeared through the hole in the ice. I thought Reber used rare restraint as well as discretion when he learned of this misfortune and passed it by without comment.

For another early errand, he sent me out for a load of hay, and the stacks were on a slope where rain and melting snow ran off. In flat country there is little need for brakes or for breeching on the harness, but in this case the ground was frozen and the grass slippery with frost. Returning, it was impossible for the horses to hold back the heavy load. Gaining momentum down the slope, the wagon slipped and slid onto the horses' rumps, pushing them along, while I continued to tug and pull on the reins. The wagon tongue and neck yoke went high in the air, the horses collars all but slipping over their heads. The frightened young horses had no alternative but to run in a mad effort to stay ahead of the big wagon that bounced in the air behind, threatening to run them into the ground.

We had almost safely reached the bottom when one horse stumbled and fell. The wagon continued over him, pushing him along until it came to a stop. As he lay motionless in a tangled mass of harness, I looked at the blood-streaked frost and snow where he had been dragged and felt certain he was dead, his bones broken, and his hide torn to shreds. In any event, I was sure he would have to be destroyed. Sadly but hastily, I got the hay out of the rack and onto the ground, wondering how to extricate the poor animal. I hitched the other horse to the rear of the rack where I had lashed a singletree. After considerable effort, we were able to pull the wagon back.

The fallen horse, spurred on by his frightful experience, got up, looked around in a daze, and began to walk about with a limp favoring his badly bruised side. It was best to keep him moving before he stiffened. Leaving the rack, we walked slowly home, and the badly limping horse made it on his own power. Reber was in the house with Belle but came out to meet me.

"You sent me out without breeching," I began.

Reber, making no comment, left me to choke on what I was prepared to say next. He went to the house for warm water, washed off the horse's lacerated hide, and applied salve.

Taking another team, I walked back to get the rack and took my time reloading the hay, for the horse's accident had shaken me considerably.

Hoping nothing else would go wrong, I was already looking forward to the end of the month, expecting to quit or be fired. Only a few days later, however, with another load of hay I encountered a stray herd of steers. Maddened by hunger, seeing my rack, and smelling the hay, they milled around on the other side of the gate I would have to go through. Bawling and butting each other, they fought for positions close to the fence where they pressed together in a solid mass of steaming hides.

I sat on top of the load for awhile trying to figure out some alternative to opening the gate, but when I concluded there wasn't any way I knew I'd have to move fast.

They poured through like a flood at a broken dam! I scarcely had a hand up on that rack when below me was a sea of horns, heads pressed together, some pulling at the hay, others chewing wildly, those farther back roaring and bellowing trying to jump over the ones in front. I didn't get any of the hay through the gate, and I felt lucky to be able to inch the horses around to where I could toss the hay off onto the prairie, a few forkfuls at a time, until I got the herd scattered.

When I got back, Reber and I caught up a couple of saddle horses and tried to round up the cattle and drive them out of his hay meadow, but we had to wait until all the hay was consumed before we could get those half-starved beasts to move. Reber must have received a satisfactory settlement for the hay because, after riding out to see the owner, he came back in a cheerful mood.

"You wouldn't want to quit now," said Reber when my month was up. "The worst is over. We've got the horses in the barn."

He may have been right in a way. To this point, it had been one fight after another. Reber and I had been dragged, trampled on, and kicked. I had rope burns, bruises, a hip pointer where I braced the rope, and had lost some of my toenails. Each night I fell onto my bunk thoroughly exhausted and the next morning I awakened with aches and pains. My torn clothes were saturated with sweat and corral dust. Pearly Gates had said it would be rough, but I was sure he didn't know how rough; no one could unless he had done it.

Nor were the horses having an easy time. We were their mortal enemies, and regardless of whether it was our lives and limbs or theirs, they wanted to be free. Getting their forefeet to the top rail of the corral as they tried to jump over, they fell backward, rolling and squealing, emitting air. Weakened by a refusal to eat, one fine big bay died of pneumonia after I had sat with him most of two nights keeping him covered with warm blankets. A young mare caught her leg in a loop, twisted and fought until it was broken, and she had to be destroyed.

Reber always left the most disagreeable work to me and took Belle into town while I dragged the carcasses down into a draw, adding them to the ones already there in various stages of decomposition.

Getting the horses into the barn was by far the most difficult task, as Reber said, but once they were in, all hell broke loose. The wild one's whole world had closed in on him, and he crouched so his belly almost touched the ground. With every muscle trembling, he was in his moment of greatest terror, intensified by his own crashes and squeals and those of others in his position.

At night I lay awake in my bunk, hearing the wild hoofs beating, the screams, and crashes, wondering what havoc they were raising. Going in before daylight with a lantern, I might find one with his head twisted back to one side, the halter rope taut, his body hung over the manger. In spite of the heavy copper riveted halter and double rope, one horse broke loose and attemped to jump through a small window through which we pitched manure. With his head and one leg through, his position was such that he could move neither forward nor back. Before we could saw a hole large enough to free him, he appeared all but dead with his eyes bulged out and his tongue hanging limp.

I never entered a horse's stall without some fear. Some tried to bite, others struck out with a forefoot or hindfoot, and a few attempted to crush me against the stall. Every day I had to go into each stall to untie the horses and lead them to the water tank. As difficult as this proved to be, it was most exasperating when some, frightened by the movement of their reflections in the water, refused to drink. Sometimes one would put his mouth to the water and jump away as though it had bitten him. I soon learned to hold the rope short, stay at the horse's side, and hang on when he reared; in that way I was safe from his hoofs and couldn't be dragged. After days of patience, slow movements, soothing voice, and gentle pats, they began to respond.

Most became tamed eventually, but a few never did. With the more difficult ones, we had to use a more forceful method, a "double U" cinch made of stout straps with an iron ring buckled onto each ankle. A rope tied to a bellyband ring was strung through the ankle rings; when pulled, it collapsed the horse's legs under him. This method had its dangers because the weight of the horse might snap a leg. Fortunately, after a few falls the recalcitrant ones stopped trying to kick things to pieces.

The results of our hard dangerous work began to show. Our horses, shedding their winter coats, were growing sleek and fat, and their combed out manes and tails glistened in the sunlight. I felt good that the worst was over and spring was on the way.

We gave the horses descriptive names. Fat Flora was a shiny black roly-poly with a well-shaped head and small feet. Gray Captain, whose name we shortened to Gray Cap, was a dapple-gray with a long barbed wire scar across his chest. He was comparatively easy to tame and may have been caught once before. Black Knight, a young black stallion with a white star, was big-boned, wide-chested, and destined to be a plow horse because his hammerhead made him unsuitable for the city. Kit and Kate, sorrel look alikes I named after Pa's Omaha team, would be suitable for a buggy or a light delivery wagon. Wild Bill and John L.

would need to be worked hard, for a day's rest inspired them to run away or to try to take things apart.

Reber began selling the horses, one by one or as a team, to farmers or to other buyers who came to look them over. Magnifying the slightest imperfections, all haggled over prices: "The horse with the scar is blemished," "This one has the heaves," "That one has carney—see his coated tongue," "Too much for a cribber," and "He's stringhalted."

Some of it was true, but they were buying for resale. Horses were required everywhere there was work to be done. A number of horse stories enlivened conversations, such as one about the farmer complaining that the dealer had sold him a blind horse.

"Now, what makes you think that horse is blind?" questioned the dealer.

"Because he runs into fences—tries to go into the barn when the door's closed—things like that."

"Heck," said the dealer, "That horse ain't blind. He just don't give a damn!"

All of these horses, fresh from the wild, were never really tame. No one knows how many became runaways, or how many wagons were wrecked and lives endangered. I remembered well our own experiences with the horses we got from Jupe, and I had heard similar tales from others, for no one can foresee how they will turn out when broken to the harness. Each one is a character with his own virtues and faults; they are as varied as human beings.

HOME FOR A REST

IT WAS EARLY spring, winter was slowly losing its grasp, and warming days followed freezing nights. Young mares Reber had kept to add to his brood string reveled at the end of the tether when taken out for their daily exercise, finding remaining drifts of snow to kick about with their newly acquired grain-fed energy. Either in play or out of pure cussedness, Nellie, one of a matched team of sorrels, would charge at me, ears laid back, as though to run me down. At the last moment she veered aside to brush by. As she grew bolder and came closer and closer, I tapped her across the nose with the quirt. Stopping short, she gave me a look of defiance and pawed the earth while shaking her creamy forelock and mane. Lady, her teammate, complemented her with a gentleness that did credit to her name.

The warm days proved less a boon when the winter's accumulation of manure began to thaw and had to be hauled out to be spread upon the land. "The Lord in his infinite wisdom found a use for it," Reber said, but the steaming fumes of ammonia scalded and blistered my feet so badly it was almost impossible to wear shoes.

I had long wished to go home for a rest to ease my numerous aches. This was an opportune time, and I had a legitimate reason. Reber recommended treating my feet with Bismuth Tannate powder and was more than agreeable that I take the buckboard with Nellie and Lady, for he wanted them broken to the harness.

"Drive them hard," he said as I started out, knowing full well that to drive a bronc team at all was a task in itself.

My ride home proved a long one, bumping along first to one side of the road, then to the other, as the horses carefully avoided the traveled path. I had little time to enjoy a warm wind that blew gently from the south or to take pleasure from observing the shimmering greens and browns of mallard ducks rising out of the cool mist that hung over the ponds formed by melting snow. The ducks flew so low I could almost touch them with the buggy whip.

It was good to get home; it seemed as though I had been gone a long time, especially because our family was not inclined to write, not even to answer the one letter I had written shortly after I left.

"We thought you would be coming home," Ma said, and everyone nodded agreement. The only news was that my first employer Sy Singer was dead.

"Fanny shot him!" Agnes blurted.

"She did not, nitwit," Ed corrected. "It was an accident."

Murder or accident, the sudden news was a shock. The rest of the family, however, was able to supply the details, or at least as many as were known to anyone. Sy had been celebrating the prospect of his getting the patent to his homestead, the place that had meant everything to Fanny. He had sold his horses, cows, and most of his other belongings, and let word get around that the farm was for sale.

I could see where that left Fanny. In her whole life she had never been farther than Vega, and after she moved to the homestead, no one ever saw her leave the place. As for being part of the community, she was "nonexistent." I could easily imagine her thoughts: what would she do, faced with leaving the homestead and her dream, "the little lake" where "the little girl" had roamed and played and someday would build her house? To me it would not have been surprising if she had caused Sy's death. Those who knew Sy preferred to believe that, in an unsteady moment after a bout of drinking, he accidentally shot himself while taking his rifle from its scabbard.

The question about his death could not be settled by Fanny since she had not spoken a word since it happened and had to be taken to the mental hospital at Yankton. I knew Sy had considered the homestead only a means to something better he had in mind for himself. He had plans for the $5,000 he figured he would get when he sold out. I resolved that on my first trip to Vega I would visit his grave, which turned out to be a mound of gray gumbo in a barbed wire enclosure in a windswept corner of Fousek's pasture. There was no marker, nor was it as yet outlined with field stones as it would be after the Fousek children herded cows there during the coming summer.

"And Jimmy Havlik killed Shepsie," Agnes continued with the news as tears welled up in her eyes. "I hate Jim. He should know the difference between a dog and a coyote."

"He sure should," I agreed. "He had a coyote for a pet. Remember that coyote pup he worked so hard to catch—Kutchko? The one that broke away and kept coming back stealing chickens in daylight, and Mrs. Havlik handed me the gun when he was taking off with a squawking chicken and ordered me to shoot? Jim was angry about it, and everyone felt he had a right to be."

"What's an old coyote compared to Shepsie?" complained Agnes. "I hate Jim."

Agnes was right, of course. The dog had been her constant companion, and at times on the lonely prairie herding cattle she must have thought of Shep as her only friend.

"We have good news, too. Tell him," Ed said, looking toward Nick.

Nick smiled, his face lighting up. "We got the flax threshed." He spoke with a tone of satisfaction, as though he had known all along it would get done. "I met Big one day down at Fouseks. We were talking about baseball when he offered to bring his rig over and 'knock out that flax.' "

"Had it mildewed much?" I asked.

"No," Nick answered, "you did a good job of stacking. There was a little mildew at the bottom, around the edges, but we're ahead by the delay—eighty-five cents a bushel more than we'd have got last fall. I feel well paid for shoveling all that snow from the stacks."

"That flax field made a lot more than you get working out," Ma said, looking at me closely. "You're not going back, are you? You look tired—your face is so drawn. No, you're going to stay home and give your feet a chance to heal." Ma was horrified at the sight of my feet.

"As soon as they're better, I have to go back, Ma. I have Reber's horses. Besides, I promised to help Reber round up another string. It will be our last chance; grass will be getting green, and the wild ones will be heading for the hills."

Ma protested, "That work is too dangerous."

"It is a bit dangerous," I admitted, "but it doesn't draw any more blood than a plow handle snapped under the jaw." One can hardly compare plowing to horse wrangling, but I was anxious to finish the season with Reber and knew I had to minimize the conditions to satisfy Ma.

"Do you get enough to eat?" she asked as we sat down to a platter of sauerkraut banked by thick spareribs.

"No, I usually leave the table hungry—as you used to say we should, during our lean years. Two halves of a canned peach and a cookie for desert; I could eat a whole can and a whole loaf of that warm bread. The place is alive with pigeons that foul the hay, but Mrs. Reber won't allow one to be killed, nor will she let me shoot ducks or prairie chickens. She doesn't even know that Reber has a gun. The day I had to shoot a horse he took her to town so she wouldn't know."

Ma took delight in seeing me enjoy the meals she prepared. She always seemed to feel that her cooking might not be as good as I had been getting at any of the places away from home. In every case, it really was as good except for the coffee. I preferred real coffee to the kind we had at home. Even now, when we had enjoyed a good year, Ma still roasted barley in the oven. How it smoked and smelled up the place! Barley coffee is bitter, no matter how much cream you add. Everyone who ever ate at our house gave a surprised look and grimace when Ma served the coffee. "Kneipp coffee" she called it, after some health concoction the German grocers stocked in Omaha. Regardless of the coffee, it was good to get enough to eat and to enjoy Ma's good solid food that stuck to the ribs.

Nick agreed to drive to Kimball with me one day. Pa kept saying we should take a good team and what was Reber thinking about giving me a couple of broncs. I had to remind him it was all part of the work and that I was getting paid for driving them.

Ma looked at them and commented, "They're probably no worse than the horses Jupe palmed off onto us."

Starting out with Nellie and Lady, we followed a zigzag pattern across the prairie until we got to the main road with wire fences on both sides much of the way. The young mares went into a panic while passing a four-horse-drawn freight with its canvas top flapping. The sting of the fence barbs sent them off in a frenzied gallop I was unable to control because the reins on one side had caught under the neck yoke. Traces worked loose from the singletree, and the light buckboard bounced crazily down a long slope. At the bottom was a narrow bridge. Trusting to the instinct of the horses, we held on; for a moment we both wished we hadn't. Instinct did get them across all right, but they hadn't allowed for the wheels, which seemed to be over the edge, floating on air.

After running themselves out, they stood, muscles quivering, until we got the tugs fastened and the harness adjusted. As usual, after such an experience, I had to part company with my stomach.

"You have to be brave to want to work with such animals," Nick said.

"Or maybe just stupid," I suggested.

It was usual for town kids, dressed in their knickers, white shirtwaists, black ribbed stockings, and high-buttoned shoes, to look upon country kids as less than equal. This was the situation even in a small town like Kimball, and it was obvious we had come in from the country. Seeing that our team was skittery, some of the kids on the street shouted and waved their arms to send the horses on another run. After getting them calmed down again and into the livery stable, we walked around town unsuccessfully looking for the kids.

Pearly Gates was glad to see me and was proud he had been instrumental in my getting the job resulting in such fine horses. "Sort of makes up for that Schulty deal," he said. Neither of us had heard anything from, or about, the Schultys since. We both wondered what had happened to them and agreed, "Probably nothing good."

My week of rest at home slipped by all too rapidly. I gained weight and my sore feet responded to the treatment Reber had recommended. The Bismuth Tannate powder had turned the skin into a brown leather, dry and hard. Nellie and Lady, now gentle as kittens, made their way back over seemingly familiar ground.

Upon my return I learned I had acquired a temporary bunk mate, Vinnie Gregg, who was not entirely unknown to me. Reber seemed happy and told me, "Vinnie will give us a hand with the roundup."

Tall, lean Vin was in his early twenties and known to me both by sight and reputation for being a wild rider. I had seen him gallop through a flock of chickens in a farmer's barnyard, scattering them squawking in all directions, frightening the wits out of the children. I had heard of his thundering by a group of girls of the Busy Fingers Sewing Circle as they sat on a grassy slope of the river bank. Riding back, he roped one, dragging her off a short distance. As she cried in fright and anger, he apologized with "I'm sorry, honey. I didn't mean no harm. I picked you out as the prettiest of the lot."

It was like him to be riding with us "just for the sport of it." I thought money couldn't have been the object for him since his brother-in-law owned a prosperous cattle ranch in an adjoining county. Like all cattlemen, they had no love for wild horses and would like to have seen them exterminated, considering them as predatory as wolf packs. They maintained, moreover, that one horse ate more than twice what one cow did and, unlike cows, which have no upper teeth, nibbled the grass right down to its roots and pawed the ground until it lay bare. Horses also charged through cattle, trampled calves, and stampeded the herds; but ranchers claimed their worst habit was that of luring domestic horses to live the useless wild life of running the range.

Vin scorned the kind of horse I rode, calling it a splayfooted goat. Granted it wasn't so good as his, for there wasn't a horse in the whole county that was Prince's equal.

"Want to ride Prince?" he asked one day.

How could I refuse after having seen him trot as though on springs, leap over any object in his path, slide down cutbanks on his rump, and weave in and out as we herded the wild ones.

Prince and I were going along a flat at a good lope when he suddenly sprang to one side. So unexpected it was that I just did manage to get two fingers around the saddle horn in order to save myself from a fall. I knew Prince was not that kind of horse! Reining him around and back, I found a rattlesnake coiled on the horse path where a moment before it may have been stretched out in the warming sun.

"What do you think of the Prince?" asked Vin proudly when I got back.

"He spooks at snakes;" I replied, "tried to unload me smack dab on top of one."

Vin counted the rattles, a meaty part of the snake still attached. "Hm!" he said, "A big one, twelve and a button."

I accepted the return of my trophy and placed it with others in my Birdseye matchbox back in the bunkhouse.

"BLAZE"

A NEW WILD STRING was in the corrals, though fewer this time. They were cautiously picking at a little hay and timorously drinking from troughs. When the sport of rounding them up was over, Vin had gone home, leaving Reber and me with the tiring and frustrating task of taming. We faced a repeat performance of flailing hoofs, grunts and squeals, hard falls, stalls kicked to pieces, and casualties to be dragged away and dumped into the draw. At one point I feared that I, too, might become a casualty when my mount, betrayed by ice hidden under dry grass, took a heavy fall, pinning my leg under

him. I had seen cowboys with permanently injured joints resulting from such falls: "ankylosis," Reber called it, knowing the
medical term. "Keep moving it," he warned, "work it out." It
pained for days, and the swelling subsided ever so slowly.

During my recuperation I spent a great part of my time trying
to bait a certain horse into captivity and was overjoyed when I
finally succeeded, much to my own surprise and Reber's disbelief.
He had failed the two preceding years, and indications this year
were that this was one horse destined to remain free. The second
time he had got away Reber shouted angrily: "You catch that
damned roan, you can have him!" Damn was a cuss word for him,
and it wasn't like him to give anything away. Could it be that he
guessed the roan couldn't be caught or wasn't worth catching, I
wondered. But Reber knew horses better than that, so I figured it
was because he was tired from our day's work.

We had expected the wild horses to be pretty weak following
the unusually hard winter, but they had given us a merry chase
over wild country, across rocky ridges, through icy streams and
brush-tangled coulees, crisscrossed by trails known only to them
and other animals just as wild. We had kept on at a relentless
pace, not stopping to eat and changing horses only twice. The two
part-coyote dogs that started out with us had long since trotted
off for home and were probably asleep somewhere around the
barn.

When at last we had gotten the band of wild horses into flat
country, we forked some hay and stationed a few tame horses to
serve as decoys, hoping the wild ones would join them. We knew
tame ones would spook at the sight of the wild horses and head for
the corral, for every horseman knows that even rested gentle horses
will spook at the sight of riders coming toward them with a band
of strange ones. If we were lucky, the wild would follow and be
led into the corral. Sure enough, heads and tails went up! Pointed
ears and distended nostrils told us we might expect more hard
riding to get even the tamed decoy horses into the corral they
had been in a hundred times.

It was a beautiful, thrilling sight when they began to swing
and swerve behind Reber. I stayed in a slow trot, well back, to
guard the rear. Soon we had them, the smell of oats gaining their
attention as they went through the gate. Reber started swinging
the long rope to swing the corral gate to. The band panicked to
the far end of the corral—that is, all except one, the roan. He flew
past Reber and came pounding back to pass me.

"Let him go!" Reber shouted in disgust and anger. "Let him go!"

"He's gone," I said, almost helplessly, under my breath. No one could have stopped him. Had Reber seen those flailing hoofs and the hate in those brown eyes? Next thing I knew, Reber was angrily shouting, "You catch that roan, you can have him!" Wouldn't I like to! I wanted a horse so bad I could taste it.

Reber looked over the catch. "A fine looking bunch of coyote bait," he mused. There were bays, blacks, buckskins, and browns, shaggy manes and tails full of cockleburs, and hoofs worn to the quick from pawing snow and the frozen ground for a few spears of curly grass. A few would be turned loose. There was a hammer-head, a broomtail, and one with a blinded light blue eye. A couple of scrawny ones whose ribs showed plainly as they stood sprattled, heads hanging, ready to fall, would be full of fight again tomorrow.

At first I gave no thought to the roan. He was usually hanging around close by each morning when I drove down to the corral with hay and water. He began to get bold after I left some oats for him near the corral. Reber wouldn't have liked that, had he known; there were a lot of things he didn't like. The horses in the corral were getting over their fear and had begun to nibble at the hay and to drink a little water, but the roan ate everything in sight. It got so that whenever I came with feed he would hightail it around at a light trot, a rocking chair lope, then a swift run with a sudden stop and haughty pose that spelled out "Just try to catch me!"

While the others were eating at the far end of the corral, I opened the gate each morning hoping he would go in. I even stopped feeding him. Finally one day a mare nickered and he went through, ever so cautiously at first, then with a burst of speed.

Reber couldn't believe it. I don't think he ever really wanted me to have that horse. We couldn't tell how old he was until we could get a closer look at his teeth. Reber guessed about seven or eight years. He admitted the horse had good shoulders, high hips, and a nice looking head. "Might make you a good horse," he said, "if you can stay on him. Won't know how he will turn out until after he is gelded."

I had to subdue my enthusiasm, but I could hardly sleep thinking about how I would get him quickly tamed, then go about riding him. For want of a better name, I called him Blaze for the way he looked when the sun shone on his mottled coat and because he had a white blaze on his forehead that whirled out from the center like a cowlick.

Horses know when you like them. After he got so I could touch him, I petted Blaze a lot when Reber wasn't around. Reber was always in a hurry, and we had to work from daylight to dark with those horses, getting them tamed and groomed to sell. There were between twenty-five and thirty horses to be fed, watered, curried and trimmed, manes and tails combed out, some driven, and others exercised. All the while they were fighting us, pulling and plunging. Every day was hard work, full of danger, and there was also the barn to clean.

After giving Blaze the usual treatment of letting him run with an old saddle on his back, which he fought the same as the rest of them, I prepared to ride him. He had a cold gleam in his eyes as if he were counting on another fight.

Stepping up into the stirrup, I loosened the rope, talking to him softly all the while, hoping he would be peaceful. It seemed too good as he trotted beautifully out of the corral looking at some wild flowers. Then he clamped his tail, did a few stiff-legged little jumps, dropped to his knees, got up, trotted a little way, and started to nibble at green grass. I thought of how we had worked so long in corralling and taming him and of how little value Reber had initially placed on him. As a judge of horses he was undoubtedly right, had it not been for all the time and effort, unwarranted as Reber thought, that I had put in. But Blaze's redeeming feature was that he was mine.

One Saturday night I rode him home. He fought the bit trying to spit it out and pranced sideways so much that by the time we arrived he was frothy wet. Sunday we rode back in a rocking chair lope as nice as you please, and I knew I had "a hundred dollar horse" if there ever was one. I knew if Reber ever wanted Blaze back, he would find something in the Bible he could quote, but I aimed to keep my horse.

Blaze gave me some near misses and did pile me once, but ownership of the horse gave me a freedom I had not known before. I looked forward to each Sunday, which had always been my favorite day anyway, for I could ride off in any direction—away from Reber's. After chores were done and the Rebers had gone to church, I rode off somewhere, anywhere, exploring places I had never seen, searching for agates, watching little live things that were unafraid, knowing the joy of finding a blossom growing alone on some rocky slope where, obviously "full many a flower is born to blush unseen and waste its sweetness. . . ."

There was a beauty in the loneliness of the prairie. How surprising it was one day to find hoof prints in an unlikely place. I followed as they led around an almost imperceptible slope, on through a narrow defile, and into a small pocket that a person seated on a horse could just see out of to observe if anyone were near.

There were five or six Indians in that pocket and they appeared to be as startled as I. Why would anyone be in such a remote, obscure place? They must have wondered what a lone rider was doing there, and how I found it. There was no raised palm, no sign of welcome, not even after I recovered enough to say, "How!" One of the men had grasped the bridle of my horse, and there were quizzical looks.

Would they, I wondered, be willing to accept a weak explanation? "I was just out for the ride," I began and checked myself before adding "looking for cattle or horses" because we all knew there were none for miles around. "I'm looking for Red Hail," I said instead, perhaps shakily, praying for time to collect my wits.

A few words in Crow dialect were exchanged, and I wished I could understand them.

"Why you want Red Hail?" the Indian who held my horse's bridle asked.

"He's my friend. We play ball. I thought he maybe be here with you. If he not here, I go."

Oh, Boy! I'm getting out of here. I touched a spur to Blaze and the Indian released his hold. I hoped they hadn't noticed that I had observed a piece of tent canvas covering what may have been a steer in the process of being skinned.

"They're gone by this time," Reber said, when I told him of my discovery. "You could have been shot," he continued—half in jest, I hoped.

As the slopes turned to shades of velvety green, warm breezes caressed the land as newborn colts frisked about in the sunshine. Spring is breeding time, and Reber informed me that a Saunders man was due to arrive with Rajah. The prospect of seeing The Duke again did not leave me overjoyed. He, too, would remember we had never been on the best of terms.

Riding in at noon a day or two later, I blinked twice at the dejected figure seated on a sunny log by the barn corral. His distinctive black cowboy hat was pulled down over his eyes, his head was resting on his arms over his knees, and the familiar silver inlaid spurs formed a contrast to well-worn scuffed boots. No picture of my old bunk mate Al would be complete without his ever-present horse Drago, named no doubt for his Drag V brand and the outfit Al had worked for before coming south to stop at the Saunders's. Drago, contentedly eating hay, looked up and nickered when I approached, but Al made nary a motion.

"Well, doggone if it isn't the tumbleweed kid!" I greeted him. Getting no response, I walked nearer. "It's me, Al."

He gave me a sullen glance through the slit of his right eye. "I knew you were here."

It was a cool reception after we had not seen each other for over a year. "What's eating you?" I asked.

"That Bible pounder you're working for—'No smoking around the barn,' he says, and I'm nowhere near the barn—the bastard!"

With no further words, I sat down on the log beside him. Intending to antagonize him a bit, I slowly extracted the makings from my shirt pocket, blew a leaf from the book of cigarette papers, tore it off, made a trough into which I poured a mound of Bull Durham, leveled it out, rolled the paper, ran my tongue along the edge, twisted the ends and, striking a match on the seat of my pants, put a light to it. I took an especially long drag and blew the smoke his way. His disgusted look made me laugh so hard I almost choked.

"That's the longest I've ever seen you without a cigarette in your face," I said, tossing the makings to him. "Here, pal, roll yourself a coffin nail. Reber and his wife drove out an hour ago. What's new at the ranch?" I asked cheerfully, hoping to get his mind off Reber, but Al wasn't one who could overlook an affront easily.

"I'm going to make that bastard put double U cinches on those mares. Can't be having no two-bit broncs kicking a thousand-dollar stud."

"Rajah?" I asked, surprised. "Oh, you mean The Duke is here this week with the stud?"

"Duke, hell!" he exclaimed. "The Duke didn't return this season, and I have to stand the stud. I don't like it one bit . . . have to get out early in the morning and then sit around and wait 'til evening. This job The Duke had was no good. It's a goddamn drag!"

"Forget those double U's," I interrupted him. "You know who would have to rig them, don't you!"

His expression brightened as he said, "I have a bottle; I'd offer you a drink, but that bastard would sure as hell complain to Mr. Saunders. I'm sure gonna punch that bastard before I leave for Texas." Al was always punching someone in talk, but never actually following through unless he was too drunk to be effective.

"Didja hear about Sy?" Al asked, and I nodded. "Sis is going to get the homestead."

"Sis?" The news startled me.

"Yeah, Fanny's been sent to Yankton, and the homestead's owner is 'Fred Saunders, guardian for Mary Saunders, a minor.'"

I felt bad about Sy and Fanny. Sy I had liked in spite of his shortcomings, and Fanny—I thought of Fanny, her little cabin, the "little lake" and how she had talked of it, dreamed about it, and the house she would build there someday. The beautiful site was now Sis's. It, too, was going from Fanny, the Indian girl who had so little, to Sis, the girl who had everything and to whom all things came so easily.

"How is Sis?" I asked, as the conversation had moved to my main interest at the Saunders Ranch.

"I don't know nothin' about Sis, never hardly ever see her. You'd do well to come and see for yourself; go back to work for Saunders." It was an opening he had evidently wanted and continued, "Anyone who would work with these bone busters," looking toward the broncos, "has got to be loco! You can have my job, nothing to do but sit around."

It was clearly evident that Al didn't like being stud man, which, of course, really wasn't a job for anyone who couldn't read. With one service in the morning and another toward evening, it made a long day but had been ideal for The Duke, studying as he was to become a solicitor—or was it a barrister—which he probably was by this time. I thought of all the books I would like to read. "I'd like the job, Al, but Saunders fired me, remember?"

"He never did fire you," Al insisted, "he says you quit. Hell, I've quit a couple of times, and Saunders says to me 'Al, all you need is dehorning, you'll be back.' He's a good guy; you'll never work for a better one."

After discarding our cigarette butts where Reber wouldn't find them, we started for the porch where our noon meal had been left, stopping on the way to water Rajah and give him his gallon of oats. As I called him "Rajah," Al snorted. "You're as bad as The Duke—his name is Roger."

I offered to bet that the handbills in his saddle wallet spelled "RAJAH."

"English talk," he scorned. "The Duke tells the printer his name is 'Rajah' and that's the way it comes out."

"You might be right," I agreed. "I think I like Roger better anyway. Good old Roger!" I said, patting his massive neck and shoulders.

When Al returned the following week, he fairly burst with enthusiasm, telling his good news: "Mr. Saunders says you can come back anytime you want to. He would even ask you to if it weren't for taking a hand away from another fellow." The possibility of Reber overhearing precluded further conversation, and I promised Al I would think about it. For some time the thought kept me awake at night and occupied my mind during working hours. I considered all the good points. It would be nice having Al as a bunk mate again and to ride out after cattle. I hadn't read a paper for months, and no doubt Mr. Saunders would again share his with me. There probably couldn't be any more "hassling" with Sis in the barn by Molly's stall since she was now a "young lady," but one could expect more of the secret "chance meetings" by the bend of the creek. The water would be high there now, splashing among the rocks, and the trees would be in new leaf, fresh and clean. We had made promises then, impossible to keep though I wished we could. Just the thought gave me a warm glow. There were many pleasant things to think about, but they always ended with the inevitable parting.

No, I could not go back to Saunders's, for I had not yet fully recovered from the last parting. It had left me lonesome and heartsick, especially in the evenings when I watched the sun set directly over where she lived. I did feel a measure of relief now to know that Mr. Saunders had said I could come back anytime I wanted to. Perhaps some day I would; it gave me a warm and comforting feeling.

How fortunate to have Blaze to whom I could transfer some of my affection. It wouldn't be manly to say I loved him but I knew I did. With one eye on Reber, I gave Blaze all of my free time, brushing, combing his long mane and tail, trimming or oiling his hoofs, giving him rewards of sugar for good behavior.

For some time I had wanted to call on the Schultys, the young couple who had been the cause of my frosted feet the previous winter. With Blaze, I now had that opportunity.

Over rough country, rocky ridges, and brush-tangled coulees I rode, thinking how surprised they would be to see me, wondering what transformation Mrs. Schulty would have effected in that bare desolate cabin that had awaited her that January day the year before. I pictured the baby, now over a year old, toddling about the little place. As the site came into view, I prodded Blaze, eager to increase the pace.

I reached the little farm only to find that it had been deserted. Pushing open the loosely hanging door, I noted that hardly a trace of occupancy remained. Even the small inadequate stove no longer stood near the center of the far wall. Evidently they had not left hurriedly and perhaps had to pack carefully for some reason. Most likely they could not afford to leave anything behind. I walked about outside, trying to reconstruct for myself the work and events that had taken place. Below the empty cabin, a small rock dam had been built. Nearby were the remains of a vegetable garden, mainly a few carrots. Happily, I discovered three very small watermelons. After my long ride in the heat of the day, I had been disappointed to find no water. I broke open one of the melons. It was still green with a show of pink, but I found it sweet and cool. A coyote a short distance away began to trot off with a side motion until, noting with the instinct known only to a coyote that I did not have a gun, he stopped and sat to watch. An owl flew past my ear as I entered the barn for a last look around. Nothing loose was lying around; most of the doors and windows of both house and barn had even been removed.

Determined to take the larger of the two remaining watermelons with me, I cradled it in one arm and began to mount. Blaze by now was a gentle horse, but he had been born wild and that wildness would forever remain within him. I had not yet settled in the saddle when he gave a mighty pitch, so unexpected that it threw me to the ground with a jolt that rattled my teeth. Blaze discovered he was loose and made his bid for freedom while I lunged to grasp hold of a rein on the ground before me. Fortunately some rocks ahead delayed his running for just long enough. The tips of two fingers reached the rein as his forefeet left the ground. The feel of the bit in his sensitive mouth brought him to such an abrupt halt that he recoiled enough for me to get a firmer hold. I was saved from an ignominious and long walk back in high-heeled boots over a tortuous path on a scorching day.

I disregarded the loss of the melon and allowed Blaze to walk slowly all the way back so I could appreciate the ride, the peacefulness and beauty of the summer day. I thought of the Schultys and how much happier they must be back in Iowa where they belonged, in the comfortable living conditions to which they were accustomed.

GOOD-BYE TO THE RANGE

SINCE MY FIRST visit home I had known Ma was anxious for me to give up horse wrangling and return to the less dangerous farm work, either at home or "working out." Reber must have had a sixth sense about my desire to leave, for each time I intended to give him notice he would give me a "partnership look" and start talking about how great the horses were shaping up and about the next phase of *our* work. Reber knew I was a good hand, and all he needed to say was, "Next week you'll be able to hitch up that team and take them out on the road."

One morning, just before haying season when farm help would be scarce, I decided it was time to quit. Conditions had become almost intolerable at the Rebers. While Blaze had made it possible for me to stand the bleak loneliness, he had been the cause of a growing alienation between Reber and me. The wrangler evidently regretted having said, "You can have that damned roan if you can catch him!"

I had admired Reber for his fearless talent with horses, his knowledge of the Bible which enabled him to quote any number of passages, and his devotion to frail, gentle Belle. I even tried to emulate the softness of his speech. Al, however, with untutored native intelligence and judgment of character, had branded him "one not to be trusted." "He's a phony, I tell ya," Al declared one day while watching Reber, all dressed up, drive out with Belle. In some respects, Al was right. Under his façade of piety, Reber gave me all the dangerous and degrading jobs, anything too disagreeable for himself. He was rousing me earlier and earlier from my sleep, long before daylight. Reber always went back to bed, and he and Belle did not rise until way past sunrise. Half-awake and aching in every muscle, I would struggle into malodorous clothing and pull my boots, stiffened by perspiration and dung, over swollen feet. As I stumbled my way to the barn, the lantern gave off the sickening odor of coal oil smoke. It was a long stretch to daybreak and the late call to breakfast, and my stomach had been without food for too long.

In my hunger, thoughts too terrible to contemplate forced themselves on me. What if, by some accident, the lantern might drop into the hay, or be kicked over, and set the barn afire? Once I had witnessed a barn fire and heard the horses' screams, almost human cries. When untied, they lacked the sense to leave; when forced out, many charged back into the inferno. For days after, I saw the charred and swollen bodies, the look of pain and terror on their faces, and smelled the stench as they were cleared away. The recollection caused me to be extra careful.

With the feeling that I had given my best, had risked life and limb, and that no man could have done more, I told Reber I was leaving. Our good-byes were cool but cordial as I picked up my pay.

I mounted Blaze and left for home, elated, knowing the family would be glad to see me. Pa would stand beside me to see how much I had grown, feel my muscles, and beam with pride. Ma always asked if I had been getting enough to eat. Everyone would stay up later than usual to talk. Riding along, I thought perhaps I should plan to stay home to help Nick with the haying and the harvest afterwards, although there were reports that crops in Brule County had not started off well and might be light.

My arrival home, unannounced, was not the grand homecoming I had envisioned. Nick, in faded blue bib denims, his shirtsleeves rolled to his elbows revealing suntanned muscular arms, gave me a wan smile of welcome and nodded, almost immediately, toward the big field adjacent to the house: "A mess, isn't it?"

"Never had a hailstorm so heavy before," he continued, "nor at a time like this when the corn was only two feet high."

I could see the tender leaves had just begun to broaden and reach out when they were cut to ribbons and pounded into the ground. Further inspection of the crops showed that the wheat, "just beginning to head and in the milk," looked almost as bad—scarcely a stalk was standing upright. As for the neighbors, the Havliks, Burians, Balsters, Kovandas, and Pitseks had all been hit, though some not so hard.

"Yes," said Pa, who had come out from the house and joined us in the field, "we will have to economize. About the only cash we are going to have for awhile, George, is what you bring in."

Grass was good on the creek bottom. I got a job haying for the Plos family one and a half miles to the north and two miles west, if one went by the section lines. They lived in a two-room cottage and lean-to, with no porch of any kind. Though cheaply furnished, the house was neat and had ruffled curtains at the windows. A few orange nasturtiums protected by chicken wire bloomed by the kitchen door, the only door in the whole house. No trees or other growth existed, for the ground was kept smooth and bare by chickens, pigs, and other farm animals. Their land was mostly either gumbo or rocky, unsuitable to farm, so their livelihood depended on a fairly large herd of cattle and a few milk cows.

Mr. and Mrs. Plos had emigrated from the province of Bohemia, as had their neighbors, and spoke only a few words of English. Mr. Plos was a small man but proud of the military bearing he had acquired as a soldier in the Austrian army. He demonstrated giving the commands, going through the manual of arms rapidly, saying "see isser quick." Past the age for heavy work, he spent his time making various items—harnesses from hides, cups from tin cans with the handles ingeniously formed of willow, a set of table knives from an old saw, a butcher knife from a file—furnishing the house with products of his skill.

Mrs. Plos was short, broad, and wrinkled, with sunken puckered lips. She usually wore a small sunbonnet even indoors, perhaps because of her sparse hair. I quickly discovered I would remember her as the world's worst cook. She fried everything in lard used over and over. One day I went out to shoot prairie chickens with every intent of having a good meal. How she succeeded in making them taste like a fried shoe I shall never know.

Mary and Wencel were the only children at home. Their older sister Annie, feeling the restraint of middle-aged parents and farm life, had left home at an early age to become a maid at the Kimball House. Although there had been fears and predictions that she would come to a bad end, she married well and was living happily in town.

Twenty-one-year-old Mary, stockily built, did most of the hard work. Her mother declared she was "a hezká dívka (pretty girl), and she never run with boys, never." I figured this may have been said for my benefit, because Mary would be working with me in the hay field whether her brother was with us or not.

Wencel, who preferred to be called "Jim," was two years younger, did not like the farm, and was home less than half the time. "Run, run, you all the time run," his father complained to him, and Mary urged, "You need to work to keep healthy and strong."

"Yes," Jim agreed, "strong under the arms." He exemplified a desire to be clean and well-groomed, dressing in his tailored clothes and sending his laundry by mail to Sioux City, Iowa. Receiving no pay for working at home, he managed by working as a part-time barber, being a pool hustler, and by playing the accordion for dances. This provided him with a top buggy drawn by the classiest trotters in the county, so he was extremely popular with the girls. To the best of my knowledge, Nora Balster was the only girl who had refused his offer to go for a drive.

Jim and I became good friends from the start, which was fortunate, because I had to share his bunk in the lean-to. It was no more than a few pine boards attached to the wall on one side and supported by narrow boards, serving as legs, on the other. It had no springs, and the mattress was a bag of corn husks. His father may have wanted him to stay home, but I slept much sounder in the hot lean-to when he was away.

Mary didn't seem to mind our having to pass through her room to get to ours. She went to bed in the dark after we had retired and was already out milking the cows by the time we got up.

The old folks slept on a pad or featherbed on the kitchen floor and had to put their "bed" down each evening and fold it up each morning.

The only newspaper in the house was the weekly *Hospodar*, a Bohemian paper that the old gentleman read word for word in the evenings while smoking his curved German pipe, drinking strong black coffee, and wiping off his long mustache. From listening to the Bohemians in Omaha and our neighbors, I had by this time learned to pronounce their words, though I did not know the meanings. When Mr. Plos discovered this, he had me read the paper to the family. Afterwards, Mary translated for me so I kept up with the news.

Mr. Plos, with Mary's translating help, told me much about his old country and about the early days in South Dakota. It intrigued him to think they were the first to live on this land, the forerunners of generations to come. He touched only briefly on the hardships they had endured and did not mention the personal misfortunes: children that did not survive the rigors of pioneer life and died in infancy, and their little boy who was drowned in the dam even before it was completed. I had seen the little cross, not far from the house, where the wild pasque-flower, or Easter flower, which has since been named the state flower, grew. He preferred to remember and tell of happy times, concluding, "I cannot think of another place in the world I would rather have come to. We had our good times and our bad, but whether it was adversity or prosperity we all shared with each other. Here there is no intolerance, no pity, and no false pride—it has been a good place for our children." I thought of Annie living in her big house in town, Mary loving the farm and being happy there, and Jim who, in spite of all the grumbling, brought light to the old man's eyes whenever the trotters came down the lane. "Jim smart," the father said. "Some day he be governor."

I smiled, for I knew the Plos family had to be capable or they would not have survived to become successful homesteaders. Their self-reliance and confidence had been demonstrated when I injured my foot shortly after arriving. Mary had insisted I see her mother who would take care of it. I had been unloading hay, pitching it up to Mary on the stack when her jacket fell, frightening the horses. As they lurched, I tried to keep my balance. One of the tines of my pitchfork went clear through my foot behind the second and third toes. Telling me that a wound of that kind, if not treated, often results in lockjaw, Mrs. Plos squeezed out as much blood as she could, washed the wound with soap and water, and poured undiluted carbolic acid into it. The acid burned like fire and seared the flesh white. For days after, it was real sore. I learned later that she had followed the proper course for those times, and I certainly had reason to be grateful.

A few days before the Fourth of July, Mr. Plos, proud to be a citizen of such a great country, announced that we should all take the day off to celebrate at the fair. It was the busiest season of the year and a period when a storm could come up any day and spoil much of the hay, but the whole family looked forward to the day and going to the fair. Jim left first with his trotters to pick up his new girl. Mary packed a lunch, hitched a team to the old spring wagon, and with an American flag flying from the buggy whip, she and the old folks were off. With Blaze saddled and ready, I mounted and followed. We were all on our way to celebrate America's birthday.

GANNVALLEY FAIR

THE ONLY TOWN on the eighty-mile stretch of dirt road from Kimball to Miller (and the only town in Buffalo County) was Gannvalley, the county seat. Known for miles around for its Fourth of July celebrations, the town itself wasn't much—a dozen dwellings, a church, and a school were scattered about as though tossed from a giant dice box. There was uniformity only in the low, false-fronted business buildings—a general store, livery barn, fuel and lumber supply house, and blacksmith shop—joined together by a wooden sidewalk. The residents were a closely knit religious group, and visitors noted the absence of both a saloon and a pool hall.

Once a year the town came to life with the Gannvalley Fair, and everyone from miles around came to renew acquaintances, play the carnival games, and patronize the food and beverage booths. The atmosphere often became raucous, but since the church benefited from the proceeds, the villagers closed their eyes and ears, talked about the huge crowd, and agreed, "It's the best fair we've ever had."

Along with the Plos family, I had been looking forward eagerly to this celebration. I arrived just before noon when the the sun was high in a cloudless sky, and it was hot. Almost everyone was already there—a crowd close to two hundred—the largest gathering I had seen since leaving Omaha. Farmers in ill-fitting mail-order clothing walked along with their wives and children dressed in ginghams and percales made from the same bolt of cloth as papa's shirt. Friends were greeted over glasses of foaming beer and ice-cold lemonade. The younger ladies in ankle-length dresses of chambray and other light materials were resplendent with wide ribbon sashes and bows in colors complementing their flowered hats. Young cowboys, eager for some kind of action, galloped around on spirited horses. On the outskirts a small band of Indians camped in a teepee; their scrawny, undersized ponies grazed nearby fighting off flies. Bronzed squaws in shapeless dresses sat in the meager shade of squaw wagons while their dogs lay around gnawing on a few large, overripe bones they had dragged in from the prairie.

I found Al's horse Drago at a feed rack and tied Blaze alongside. I could hear Al nearby in an argument with Henry Irons, the part-time sheriff, Indian agent, and rancher who was in charge of the bronco busting contests and horse races. There had always been bad blood between the two anyway. Irons was part Indian, swarthy, heavyset, and wore a big star on his vest.

"I can ride better drunk than you can sober," Al was shouting.

"You're juiced," replied Irons, walking away.

"If there's anyone I'd like to whip, it's a sheriff," Al continued, speaking to no one in particular and taking a vicious bite of a plug of chewing tobacco. "I'll show'm!" Climbing to the top pole of the corral for outlaw broncs, he half-fell, half-jumped to the back of a mean-looking dun-colored horse. Angered and frightened, the horse bowed his back and, with a simultaneous leap and kick, sent half-seated Al sprawling in corral dust. Delighted by the impromptu performance, a lad in tight knee pants exclaimed gleefully, "He dumped ya! He dumped ya!"

"He did not!" scorned Al, angrily dusting and rearranging his clothes. "I got off. Go tell your mother she's looking for you."

"Hey, Al, let's go watch the basketball," I called to him.

Ordinarily basketball held little interest for Al, but at the moment the broncs were hardly his forte. At the roped-off area where the game, married women versus single girls, was about to begin, we were greeted casually by Mr. Oates, a friend of the Saunders. He was intent on his sprightly wife and her group, garbed in daring full-cut purple bloomers, white middies, black stockings, and tennis shoes.

"Real class," Al commented and turned to me. "Who ya bettin' on, Joe?"

The opportunity seemed too good to pass up. The bloomer girls, awkward, fat, and out of shape, didn't have a chance.

"A dollar on the singles," I replied, limiting Al's loss. I'd have bet more, but I felt no satisfaction in taking unfair advantage of him.

"Very smart," Mr. Oates approved. "I'd back them myself, if I dared."

To our surprise, however, the married women won easily. The single girls were hampered by their long dresses and could not outplay their opponents though they struggled desperately. Bess Oates stole the show as she scored with four long tosses and maneuvered her way close to the basket for two other shots. When she came over for her husband's congratulations, Al waved my dollar at her and beamed.

"That game cost me a day's pay," I muttered as we hurried toward the Congregational Church women's gaily decorated booth to order a plate of baked beans with ham hocks. Dessert was extra, so we passed up the ladies' tempting cream pie in favor of homemade vanilla ice cream, yellow as butter, at the booth of the Busy Fingers Sewing Circle. The sewing club was operating under its fancy new name, "The La Quinsan Club," which no one could pronounce. Sunbonnets and aprons for sale were on display; out of reach of inquisitive fingers was a "For Display Only" arrangement of fancywork intended for the members' hope chests. Knowing Sis was a member of this club and remembering evenings at the Saunders ranch, I could not help thinking of her pretty embroidered things a lucky guy would someday share.

"Is Sis Saunders around?" I asked the girl on duty.

"No, she'll be here this afternoon, from two to four."

The sound of drums from the Indians' encampment interrupted the conversation, and Al urged, "Let's go," for he didn't want to miss the start of the Victory, or Scalp, Dance, a name the white man didn't like, preferring to call it the War Dance. The dancing Indians seemed in earnest as the beat of the drums, the rhythmic chant, and the blood-chilling yells grew in intensity. The old Indians, wearing cast-off soldiers' uniforms of every description, were in an excited frenzy and appeared more savage than those I had seen perform with Buffalo Bill in Omaha.

When the tomahawks were swinging wildly, Vin Gregg joined in; many spectators cheered him and others held their breath. Vin chose Splitnose, grabbed a braid in each hand, and followed close behind, mimicking chant and movement. Knowing Splitnose's reputation for animosity toward the white man, I expected him to turn any minute and unleash his vengeance with the wicked-looking cavalry saber he carried, as leader, in his upraised right hand. Al agreed that taking such liberties with Splitnose could be dangerous—"or with any one of those old braves," as he put it, "for they all have one foot on the warpath and have never buried the hatchet." Most of us were relieved when the drumming ceased and the dance ended.

Al had had no liquor since being with me and by time for the bronco busting was quite sober. Irons, who had been observing him, asked, "Al, would you like to ride?"

Still feeling rebuffed by the morning encounter, Al refused, much as he wanted to get into the contests. "I wouldn't ride for that bastard now if he paid me," Al said as we walked away.

We took in the events from the top rail of the corral, and it was soon obvious that Al regretted his petulance.

"Ride'm, cowboy!" he shouted whenever a lad drew a tough one. "Let 'er buck, whoopee!" he yelled, waving his Stetson. Several times he told me, "I can do better," finally adding, "so can you. We'll have to be in there next year, Joe—only I won't be here. Be in Texas then."

He had spoken of Texas a number of times. "I'll go with you," I said, knowing I couldn't and only wishing I might.

Because of the betting, no event drew so much interest as the horse races. We had dollar bets on the first two races and broke even. The third race was "for Indians only." There were four fairly good-looking mounts and a fifth nag ridden by Wa Sau

(Grease). His horse, Fly or Horsefly, had been an old cavalry mount, and no one took his entry seriously. All five got off to a good start, but at the quarter post Fly was well to the rear. At the half, the four were nicely bunched, with Fly running along just for the heck of it. As they flashed past the third post, Fly had been forgotten. My horse was ahead by a length with Al's second, making a close race.

As the horses pounded toward the finish line, excitement was intense, with shouts of encouragement and arms waving wildly. It was too much for my horse, well in the lead; he panicked and bolted the track. The cayuse horse instinctively avoids danger by following the leader, so the other mounts followed, continuing their race across the prairie. Faithful Fly, the old cavalry charger, roared on as though he were carrying the guidon, and the bugler of the National Guard squad gave the call "Charge!" The amused crowd sent up a cheer as Fly, nostrils distended and sucking in air at every lunge, crossed the finish line. Sheriff Irons held Wa Sau's hand aloft and, with the approval of all, declared him the winner of all three place prizes—a total of $22.50—probably the most money Grease had ever had in his life.

The Indian race would have been a fitting climax to the day's racing, but Irons's voice was heard above the crowd. "Don't go away, folks," he begged. "We're going to have a special race, for ladies only."

At the track there appeared to be only one entry, Tansy Steele. A tall girl, colorfully dressed in leather skirt, red and white striped shirtwaist, with a blue scarf at her neck, she sat impatiently on her horse, a dark bay champing at the bit. Steele was her married name—she was one of the four Sperry daughters, good ranch girls and each much-liked by the boys.

Not wanting to cancel the race, Irons spotted Sis, who had just arrived from her duty at the La Quinsan booth. Although dressed in pink chambray, she acceded to his pleadings and, with the lace on her petticoat showing, brought Molly to the track.

Thinking Sis's action a bit daring, one woman commented, "She's a little hussy."

Another agreed, "She never intended to enter because this race would be too tame for her."

Their friend joined in, "If there'd been a mixed race this year, she'd have been prepared. Remember last year—she was the only girl riding against three Indians and a cowboy—that's more her style. A real hussy!"

Mr. Darby of the *Valley Weekly* silenced them with, "Any girl who sings gospel hymns with such sincerity has to be a mighty good girl."

As the girls neared the starting line, Al said, "This looks like fun. Who ya bettin' on?"

I figured Tansy Steele to win but didn't want to bet against Sis. "Who are you betting on?" I asked him in return.

"Sis," he said.

"So am I." I thought that would get me out of betting, but a squat man in town clothes, derby hat, and light checkered vest, with an unlit cigar in his mouth, asked, "How much on Pinkie?"

I was in a dilemma—I didn't want to bet on Sis. I hadn't wanted to bet at all. "Ten bucks," I answered, figuring that would scare him out.

Without hesitating, he peeled off a ten from a large roll and handed it to Al, saying, "You hold the stakes."

Dejected, I emptied my pockets. With small change I was barely able to make up the ten dollars. Al's look may have indicated approval since he seemed confident in Sis's ability, but I figured he'd never seen her ride in ankle-length pink chambray. I'd had enough of betting on fancy-dressed girls at the basketball game, so I took his look to mean "Sucker." There seemed to be little hope for my ten dollars, although there was no doubt that Sis's Molly looked the better horse. She was "squirrel light on her feet," and her entire body looked alert and eager to go.

I didn't want to be around at the finish to see Al hand the money over to the stranger, so I walked away a little distance. Both horses got off to a good start, but to my surprise Tansy's horse fell behind at the far turn. In the stretch Sis and Molly were ahead by at least two lengths when Tansy's horse came to life with an easy long stride. Each stride brought him closer until he was even with Molly or slightly ahead. I couldn't look any longer; I had too much at stake. The crowd was yelling, "They're neck and neck!" As they crossed the finish line, everyone turned to his neighbor and asked, "Who won?" I didn't have to ask—I felt I knew—and wandered off to the edge of the crowd.

Al, grinning, came looking for me almost immediately. "We won!" he exclaimed. "The judges reported Molly was the winner. We won!" He handed me the twenty-dollar stakes and proudly held up another bill. "See, I won, too." His bet had been only a dollar.

Later, we heard that Tansy claimed her horse could have won. "It was my riding—I held up until too late," she said.

With twenty dollars in my pocket, I felt it was a memorable race. Al, determined to have a drink to celebrate, hurried me to a gaily decorated beer booth. We had our beer and walked on to where a spieler was conducting one of the carnival games which consisted of a small tripod table, a few numbered octagonal blocks, and a chart with black or gold painted numbers.

"Risk a dollar, win twenty!" he was shouting.

We had been watching for awhile when a man—the one from whom I had won the ten dollars on the horse race—put down a dollar and, using the stick provided, knocked over the blocks. In the twinkling of an eye the spieler added up the total. "Thirty-two," he announced, pointing out the gold number on the chart. "The gentleman has just won twenty dollars, a golden eagle!"

Al fished a silver dollar out of his pocket and was all for risking it for an easy twenty when I pulled him aside. "The game is phony," I warned. "That fellow won only because he's a shill."

Al didn't know what a shill was but, accepting my superior knowledge in such matters, consented to stay in the background while others frittered away hard-earned dollars.

A pale young man in a white shirt and a poorly fitting light suit, carrying a violin case under his arm, had approached the game. By my count, he "risked" ten dollars without a win and was ready to quit when my race track friend again stepped forward and put down a dollar.

"Another winner!" cried the spieler, holding up a gold piece for all to see. "A golden eagle to the gentleman. Risk a dollar, win twenty, come one, come all," he called, and added softly, "Try it again, Lad," to the pale young man with the violin case. The young man did try again, and again—twenty dollars in all.

A cowboy, deciding he had seen enough, pushed the small table over with a spurred boot. The spieler, cursing him, was promptly sent to the turf by a right cross to the jaw. The shill hastily helped retrieve the scattered blocks, and the two men were off in their rented rig, stirring up dust on the road to Miller. I figured that except for the ten dollars I had won their day had been all profit.

The crowd thinned in late afternoon to return later for the evening events. Fireworks vied with the soundless flashes of heat lightning in the distance and attracted the largest crowd. Mr. and Mrs. Plos left with Mary after the fireworks, but Jim, of course, with his girl, stayed for the dance. It was held under a striped canopy with a real three-piece orchestra instead of merely a violin or an accordion so it drew music lovers as well as dance enthusiasts. A refreshment booth featuring homemade ice cream, a variety of delicious cakes, popcorn, candy, punch, and coffee furnished "supper." With gentlemen outnumbering ladies about two to one, most girls complained proudly, "I haven't sat out one dance all evening." Those who did not know how to dance and were too shy to learn looked on and listened to the music. Stags found it difficult to get dances, there were so few unescorted girls.

"I *cand* dance, but my sister *can*," one pretty girl informed me, but her sister was on the dance floor and so popular that I never got to meet her. Sis's presence was dampened for me because she was with someone else—an older man, at least twenty-five, wearing ice cream pants and a bow tie. I learned, however, that he was her cousin from Sioux City and she was seeing that he had a good time. Sis was dancing quite a few numbers with him, and for all the others she had arranged for him to dance with her La Quinsan Club friends. Since all these girls were escorted, Sis was obliged to exchange dances with their partners. I felt I had no chance with her and could not even catch her eye.

After awhile I saw Sis coming toward me and stepped aside, figuring she was looking for someone beyond me, but she placed a hand on my arm and beckoned toward the floor. The orchestra was playing "Let Me Call You Sweetheart," and I was lost in a wonderful dreamworld.

It's been a long time," she began. "You didn't want to come back to the ranch, did you?"

"If that's an invitation, someday I will," I promised.

She gave my hand an assuring squeeze when I returned her to her partner who had either picked an unattended girl or had sat that one out. After another dance with her, I rejoined the stags. Some of the fellows were getting no dances and teased, "We have one lady-killer in the crowd. How do you do it?"

When she left shortly after, the party lost most of its glow. Two women who could pass as young farm wives were alternately escorting men to their lantern-lit tent. When the sheriff chose both an opportune and somewhat embarrassing time to make a raid on their place and confiscate a horde of silver dollars, one of the women running away was heard to cry, "There goes my slipper! There goes the other! And the SOB has my money!

The entire day had been one of excitement and pleasure, perhaps the best I had ever known. When I went to get Blaze, Drago was still there, although I had not seen Al for hours. Looking around, I found him sleeping soundly in the hay. I left quietly so as not to waken him and headed back to the Plos farm.

ANOTHER HAYING JOB

FOLLOWING the Gannvalley Fair only a few days of work remained at the Plos farm. As I left, the warm, friendly family regretfully said their Bohemian good-byes, *s Bohem* and *na shledanou*. I was in good spirits after an enjoyable stay and felt lucky to be going to another job. I had tried unsuccessfully to get on with a threshing crew; everywhere I looked, headed grain in small stacks fairly shouted at me: "Poor crops! Farmers can't afford help and don't need any." Fortunately Jim Plos, in his futile attempts to court Nora Balster, had learned that her uncle August Hardwig needed a haying hand, and I had arranged to go there after finishing my job at Plos's.

An early morning sun spilled its rays over the prairie as I started out for the Hardwig ranch eighteen miles northeast at the headwaters of Crow Creek. The day, although already getting hot, was a chance for rest after my long days of toil under a broiling sun. Blaze and I loafed along until near our destination we came upon what I at first thought was a mirage. However, as we approached, it neither disappeared nor moved farther away.

"Real water!" I exclaimed, noting its cool, shimmering contrast to the seemingly endless sun-scorched prairie. Marsh grasses never looked so green, nor cattails more beautiful, as red-winged blackbirds, ever on the move, fluttered among the bobbing spikes. Ducks, their colored plumage reflecting the morning sun, rode the ripples made by a warm breeze.

The road dropped off sharply, and the clear water, about six feet deep, looked so cool and inviting I could scarcely wait until I had stripped before plunging in. A mink, almost hidden by the protective coloring of his fur against the bank, dropped in ahead of me. I could have stayed there all day and, while dressing, vowed that if I ever had a place of my own it would be in such a setting.

Receding waters had left a flat plain of powdery alkali around the shore, with small islands of wire grass here and there. Hidden under the dry alkali were treacherous wet spots of sticky gray gumbo, and when we tried to cut across, Blaze bogged down halfway to his knees and struggled to get back out. We learned it was better to use the road to get around the lake. Farther on, the road passed through a meadow of lush blue joint grass, stirrup high, and crossed a rickety narrow bridge over a little stream.

On the other side of a knoll stood a small cluster of buildings, closely grouped as one might expect in areas where land is of greater value. Unlike most buildings in that part of the country they were more permanent, built entirely of field stones except the wood upper part of the cattle barns. Small windows and thick walls rendered the buildings cool in summer and warm in winter.

The Hardwigs were strangers to me except for their daughter Edith, Mr. Balster's niece. She was the young woman with the crippled arm who had been a teacher at Ed and Agnes's school. Fortunately Edith was home when I arrived, for I would have had some difficulty conversing with the old people, *die alter,* whose German I soon discovered was different from the few words I could understand.

Both Mr. and Mrs. Hardwig were of less than average height. She, with an ample bosom and her hair in a bun atop her head, was wearing a long apron and wooden-soled shoes. He, with a heavy black beard brown-stained with tobacco juice, looked at me with shifting black eyes that seemed to pierce right through me. Although during my stay he never spoke more than a few gruff monosyllables, none of which I ever understood, he must have been a kindly man; his wife and daughter ruled with gentle hands.

Edith hopped around like an ant on a hot rock and said everyone was in an especially gay mood because she was "fixin' to get married." I had understood she quit teaching to marry the Gannvalley blacksmith; however, the wedding, the first in the family, was just now to take place, and Edith was in her early thirties.

When her brother Albert came in, I recognized him as the man with the violin case who had lost so much money in the numbers game at the Gannvalley Fair. With horse and buggy, this carelessly dressed young man drove about the country giving concerts, playing for dances, and occasionally drinking more than he should. When he came home, he was sometimes found the next morning asleep in his buggy, his horse by the haystack near the barn. In spite of being scolded often, he was the favored member of a family who never referred to him as other than *der Herrn* (the master), a pet name that Edith explained he had been called since childhood.

If the household was considered to be in a state of excitement for the approaching wedding, I wondered how quiet and dull it must be at other times. The family went to bed right after chores when it was scarcely dark and rose before daylight.

In the fields with the old folk, I thought how much easier the work could be with modern tools and machinery, as Nick had insisted upon acquiring at our place. The Hardwigs did everything the slow, hard way just as they had done in the old country.

The water which I drank by the gallon in hot weather was a problem because theirs was full of alkali and proved to be most debilitating. "You will get used to it," they promised, but I never did, and I had no desire to stay around long enough to find out when I would become immune.

Working there had many redeeming features, the best of which, of course, was the beautiful lake. Sundays and early evenings, I went there to swim, watch the wildlife, or lie in the sun. Not only was I allowed these opportunities, but the Hardwigs even urged me to go because of the ducks. How they loved those *enten,* and how amazing that, with the ducks not far from their front door, no one in the family had ever fired a gun. There was a brand new Winchester pump shotgun, bought for Albert and never used. I would have found it great sport had they been more generous with ammunition; with only three shells, it was evident that I was expected to "pot hunt or sluice 'em," as we called it.

Mrs. Hardwig put up jars and jars of duck breast in brine. Her German-style cooking was not only good but also more than ample, which is saying a lot because it seemed that I was always hungry. I enjoyed such things as pickled and smoked pork, lentils, and freshly-baked coffee cake, but best of all was the creamed tomato soup which I tasted for the first time. They also ate something called a "husk tomato," a purple-looking food that caused me to gag when it merely touched my tongue.

The job completed, I left Hardwigs with, *"Viel Glück, auf Wiedersehen"* and a feeling that I had spent those four weeks in a foreign country.

SWEET SPRING RANCH

WHEN I SAW the neat and carefully tended appearance of the Sweet Spring Ranch, I knew I would enjoy my stay there. The elaborate carved lettering of the sign over the entrance indicated the imposing style of living enjoyed by the owners, Charley and Bess Oates. The house with its gingerbread trim, flower garden, and screen porches was exactly what one might expect lovely, vivacious Mrs. Oates to have. Affluence abounded with big red barns, miles of four-strand wire on cedar posts, and fat cattle. The two little boys, Harry, seven, and Willie, four, were playfully chasing each other in some sort of game near the front of the house. The other member of the household, of whom I was to see very little, was Mr. Oates's mother, a Queen Victoria type of woman who never spoke to the help nor, for that matter, ever interfered.

I soon learned, however, that Mr. Oates had an "employer personality" that differed sharply from the congenial calm rancher I had met and talked with on several occasions at the Saunders's and most recently at the Gannvalley Fair. "The boss" had a changeable temper with the men who worked for him. Buzz Clayton, who was older, more experienced, and a top ranch hand, generally did not draw Oates's ire, but seventeen-year-old Mike Chapsky, known as "the Kid," annoyed him frequently.

Mike was getting only fifteen dollars a month and needed the job, for he and his widowed mother lived on a rock-strewn homestead and were trying to make a living with a few cows and chickens plus the boy's seasonal work. Although he tried hard, Mike was seldom able to please Oates and got into a lot of trouble, but always when everything seemed to be going fine.

One day the four of us were driving a large herd of cattle from the "north ranch" to the shipping pasture. Everything was quiet and going smoothly until we prepared to cross the creek. On a low bluff on the other side stood a surrey filled with women decked out in light summer dresses, skirts billowing and scarves waving in the breeze.

"I had the girls over," Bess explained later. "We thought it would be fun to go out and see the cattle drive."

The cattle on Mike's side spooked at the unfamiliar sight, refused to cross, and took off up the creek. Mr. Oates was shouting mad.

"What the hell do those damn fool women think they're doin'!" he shouted as he headed in Mike's direction to help.

"Head 'em, Kid! Dammit, head 'em! Why'd ya let 'em get away?"

Mike's horse wasn't equal to the task, and Mr. Oates was getting madder by the minute. Urging Mike to get going, he spurred his own horse angrily.

Meanwhile Buzz and I, holding the main herd, had all we could manage. Looking up the creek to check how the two were doing, I saw a horse stumble and go down. Both horse and rider rolled over, down the bank, and disappeared. Buzz and I both thought it was Mike.

"If that so-and-so killed that Kid!" Buzz exclaimed, deserting our post. Instinctively, I rode after him and, arriving, we found the injured rider was Mr. Oates. He was sitting up, leaning against Mike.

"My leg's busted," he said, just as cool and matter-of-fact as could be.

After Buzz and I made a splint, Bess and one of her friends drove him into Wessington Springs to the doctor. It was late by the time we rounded up the scattered herd and got them bedded down. Mike was still disconsolate about Mr. Oates's broken leg, and we had a time trying to convince him it hadn't been his fault.

"Oates was just tryin' to show off in front of the womenfolk," drawled Buzz.

"I s'pose so," Mike finally agreed, reflectively, "like the time

I wasn't mowing fast enough to suit him. He got on the mower and whipped the horses into a near trot. A calf was lying in the high grass. Before it could get out of the way or Oates could stop the team, he'd cut off its legs. I sure don't like his cussin' me, but Jeez!—seeing that calf cut to pieces! Happened 'bout three weeks ago—can't get it out of my mind."

Buzz and his wife lived in a cabin on the north ranch. Mike and I slept in the barn at the home place, which was fine with me. I liked the sweet smell of fresh hay and the comfort of the horses, but unless there was a good stiff breeze blowing the mosquitoes were awful. I never knew so many could be in one place until I walked through a marsh in the pasture my first morning to bring up the horses. I noticed the hides of Oates's horses were covered with thick welts that offered some protection, and their chief concern was blowing the pesky insects from their nostrils. Blaze's sleek hide took the full brunt, and he was black with mosquitoes so gorged they couldn't move. When I crushed them with my hand his hide dripped with blood. His nostrils, faring no better, were raw.

As each night in the barn added more and more welts, Mike and I decided to change our sleeping quarters. We discovered a couple of bunks in the loft of a little cabin used as a storeroom. It was the sort of small government-provided house that I had seen dotting the Indian reservations. The structures had been abandoned by the Indians because of some superstitious fear they could not explain—perhaps someone had died there or there were strange noises. Buzz said Mr. Oates and his first wife had lived in this cabin, and the new house was built for Bess. The attic, or loft, reached by an outside stairway, was hot and lacked ventilation so we slept fitfully at best, but Mike had less trouble sleeping than I.

One night shortly after we moved in, I heard footsteps slowly coming up the outside stairs. Apparently when they sensed detection they retreated swiftly. For awhile I scarcely dared breathe, so realizing I had to get some sleep, I got up and peered out into the moonlight, but there was nothing.

Mike, however, was sleeping peacefully. No sooner was I back in bed when there were footsteps again. Being wide awake this time, I was sure it was not a dream. Sleep finally came only through sheer exhaustion.

After a few nights of suspenseful quiet, I was again awakened by the same stealthy footsteps and shouted, "Who's there?"

Back down the stairs they went with a swish, as though of skirts. "Skirts?" I reasoned, puzzled. "A female visitor? Is it possible?"

Further intermittent visits annoyed and puzzled me, but I began to gain confidence. After all, had I not in childhood survived the bogeyman, witches, goblins, threats of punishment by both God and the devil, terrifying tales by the Sisters in Sunday school about what happens to sinners, and stories of murders and mayhem in the Bible? The haunting and frightening dangers that were everywhere ready to pounce on innocent children had not touched me, and I thought of myself as a man now, fearing neither the devil nor any ghost—if it would only show itself!

Mike was a sound sleeper until the night he too heard the footsteps. "Do you hear that?" he asked, his voice trembling. He wanted to tell Mr. Oates about the "haunts" the next morning, but I urged him not to: "It would make us look foolish."

That night he moved back into the barn. "Mosquitoes or not," he announced, "at least, I know what *they* are!"

Alone now, I borrowed a book from Bess, an old copy of *Tom Brown's School Days*. By reading awhile each evening, I found I could sleep through the night without being awakened— that is, until one night when the footsteps were louder and more determined. Waking, I noted that they seemed heavier than usual and were causing creaking sounds as well.

Breathlessly, I awaited the inevitable retreat, which failed to occur. As they kept coming, all my senses told me to get out of there, but there was no way out. Cautiously, I sat up and stared toward the screen door, just in time to see a shadow appear and a hand fumble at the latch. The rusted spring squeaked. My heart was in my mouth as the door opened and closed. Something, or someone, was in my room! The thought of a gun flashed through my mind. I was more than aware that I had none and was sure that the figure in the doorway must be armed. My heart pounded as his hand went to his pocket. I felt weak and unable to move. There was a scatching sound on the doorjamb and a match flickered and burst into flame.

"Hi, Joe," a familiar voice said.

No one but Al ever called me Joe. My fright turned to disgust mingled with anger. Still shaken, and also to gain time, I purposely had some difficulty getting my lantern lit.

With my wits together by that time, I felt annoyed partly because of the intrusion and more so because of the realization that Al, of course, was not my "regular ghost." So my mystery was still unsolved!

"You damn fool! At this hour, what are you doing here?" was the most intelligent thing I could think to say.

A bit taken back, Al started to say something about Texas, which was always his favorite subject after a few drinks. I decided that, showing up like that in the middle of the night, he had most likely been drinking, and I wasn't about to stay awake to hear more talk of Texas.

"We'll talk about that in the morning," I suggested. "Let's get some sleep." I motioned toward Mike's bed.

Al removed only his boots and crawled in. "I ought to make you sleep here," he said. "You've got my bed."

It was obvious I did have the better bed, in the better location as far as air was concerned. It may well have been "his bed," for both he and The Duke, when standing stud with Rajah, spent several days at the Oates ranch as a sort of headquarters.

I slept even more fitfully than usual and dreamed of being in a room with a ghost. Al slept soundly, which further annoyed me. It was early daybreak when I was awakened by the smell of his cigarette.

"Well, ya goin' with me?" he asked.

"Going where?" I said, blinking, half-awake.

"Texas. You know, I asked you last night."

"Texas," I echoed. Al seemed serious, but after listening to him so much in the past, I thought this must surely be more of his wishful thinking. I looked at his clothes: shiny new boots, new buckskin-colored Stetson, and Texas Ranger pants with double seat and buttonover flap pockets. Along with a neat hair trim, this outfit made him look the cowboy fashion plate. No doubt about it, he was on his way.

Al would never understand why I couldn't pick up and go with him on such short notice, nor why I should feel a sense of obligation to my family—or to anyone for that matter. "I don't have any money," I said, thinking I had a good excuse and one that he would understand.

"Who needs money?" he countered. "We'll sleep in hay piles, and farmers always like to set an extra plate—just for enjoyin' our company. When we need a couple bucks, we'll put in a day or two of work along the way. We'll get to Texas before snow flies. The Panhandle—that's where the Matador headquarters are. Con McMurray, my pa's old boss, will give us a job right off. We'll eat, come hell and high water. What say, Joe? Hot damn, free as the wind!" He emphasized his enthusiasm with a grasp of my arm.

It sounded good. How I wished I could roll up my belongings, saddle Blaze, and ride off with Al! His words tore into me as I watched him ride off alone down the lane—just Al, his horse, and his bedroll, with not a care in the world. What a wonderful life the itinerant cowboy leads! I thought of how happy the ones I had met always seemed.

One cowboy I had heard of was the young fellow with the southern drawl who stopped overnight at the Havliks. As Aaron told it, after breakfast the "guest" slipped the leftover flapjacks in his hat, and no one would have suspected had not the syrup run down his face. As the poor fellow tried to wipe it away he made it all the more noticeable—Aaron laughed, demonstrating how he tried to reach his nose with his tongue.

I remembered, too, the two fellows Karl Urban let sleep in his barn one rainy night. They had not expected an invitation to breakfast, which proved embarrassing because their shirts bulged above the belt line with eggs. One fellow's blouse failed to hold, and he suffered all through breakfast, sitting on broken eggs.

Some of the stories I heard about "the cowboy and the farmer's daughter" probably were not true, but they helped make the life seem even more glamorous.

Al by now was out of sight, though it was not too late to overtake him, see him grin, and hear him say, "I knew you'd come with me, Joe!"

I dressed slowly, with a heavy heart, and prepared to start another day of work at the Sweet Spring Ranch.

BEYOND THE HORIZON

ALL'S DEPARTURE for Texas left me inert. Time and again I wished I had been able to go with him, to continue to enjoy his friendship, cheerfulness, and carefree attitude. His "Hi, Joe" and sense of humor always made me feel good, and I greatly admired him as a cowboy. Whereas I looked perhaps too much to the future, Al's whole concentration was on the present. The range had been his whole life, even before he went to work for the Drag V at the age of eleven.

I began to think more and more about the possibility of owning a piece of land of my own someday, for I figured there would always be free land for homesteading farther west, not only in the Dakotas but also into Montana. Earlier that year the opening of land just west of the river had reinforced my ideas. New towns were springing up, and young men whom I had met and worked with were coming back for brief visits and talking of Kennebec, Presho, and Vivian, and their homesteads on or near Medicine Creek. They had gone during early spring in wagons loaded with lumber for their cabins, enough household goods for bachelor housekeeping, the necessary farm machinery to till the soil and put in a few acres of crops, and the inevitable cow trailing along behind with its rope attached to the endgate.

During visits home, they boasted of the number of acres of sod they had turned over and seeded to grain but touched only briefly on their inconveniences and hardships. Joe Pitsek, however, did mention the rattlesnake he'd found coiled in his bed, and Frank Urban told of killing eight one day with a shovel without moving out of his tracks, while preparing to dig a posthole. Since each seemed to be enjoying his experience, I felt I had something to look forward to. I could envision that like most of them I too would marry and thereby acquire a helpmate. My bride, of course, would be brave, strong, and willing to put up with all the inconveniences that were the lot of the prairie wife. We too would return for visits, singing the parodied verses and chorus of "My Little Old Sod Shanty on the Claim":

I am looking rather seedy now, while holding down my claim,
And my victuals are not always served the best,
And the mice play slyly round me as I nestle down to rest,
In my little old sod shanty on the claim.

CHORUS
The hinges are of leather and the windows have no glass,
While the roof, it lets the howling blizzard in,
And I hear the hungry coyote as he slinks up through the grass
Round the little old sod shanty on my claim.

2
Yet I rather like the novelty of living in this way,
Though my bill of fare is always rather tame,
But I'm happy as a clam, on my land from Uncle Sam,
In the little old sod shanty on my claim.

But to do this, I would have had to wait until I became twenty-one, which meant three more years of drudgery and wasted time! Besides, at eighteen, I was no longer a boy. I had already proved myself following the plow, the seeder, and the drag. I had put in crops and harvested, worked with a threshing crew, shoveled loads of grain, husked corn, put in miles of telephone line, skinned and butchered, roped and branded cattle, and tamed wild horses. There was nothing a man could do that I could not do as well. Standing still at this point seemed the equivalent of going backward, and one must go on. I knew there was something out there beyond the horizon. In song and story, men had found both fame and fortune by journeying toward the sunset star.

Back in my grammar school days in Omaha, California had been only a large colored space with an irregular outline on the large wall map of the United States. I had taken more note of that faraway state the summer of 1905, however, and my interest in going there someday had become aroused.

For many years the railroads had issued passes to politicians to use as rewards to their constituents, and in Omaha Pa had received several for short trips. Since these could be used by anyone, they had been an opportunity for Ma and one or more of the children to visit relatives. Several times some of us went to Plattsmouth, Ma's home area, where most of her family still lived, and other times we went to visit Aunt Rose in Minnesota and Aunt Mary in Plainview, Nebraska.

The summer of 1905 was different. Jim Dahlman himself, Omaha's mayor-elect, delivered the ticket, which was a yard or more long. Pa was receiving a free trip to attend the Exposition in Portland, Oregon, and to continue down the coast through California, with stopover privileges. We boys, hiding behind the big oak tree in our front yard, looked on in awe as this man who Pa had said would become mayor alighted and climbed the long stairs to our seldom-used front door. There, in the courtly manner of one serving royalty, he doffed his hat, bowed low, and handed the ticket to Ma. To all of us, it was a day to remember.

How proud, dignified, and important Pa looked a few days later as he departed, attired in a new cassimere suit, Homburg hat, shiny congress gaiters, and wearing across his ample girth his heavy gold watch chain with the lodge emblem on the fob. We watched with pride as he crossed the vacant lot and disappeared from sight beyond the slippery elms and black walnut trees along the road to the streetcar.

Ma felt the pressure of sole responsibility of running the house and looking after boys aged fourteen, twelve, and nine, and four-year-old Agnes. As days ran into weeks, postcards arrived depicting the beauties of an unbelievably fabulous country of flowering fruit trees, sandy beaches, and a blue ocean.

When Pa returned after a month and a half, we scarcely recognized him, for his hair and mustache were dyed black! "A silly caprice," Ma proclaimed, "that we can ill afford."

Over "Red Dago" wine, which he had had shipped home and shared with his friends, we listened as he told of orange groves, grape vineyards, highways lined with palm trees, and white yachts sailing on a blue bay.

"Why," I asked him, "doesn't everyone go there?"

"Money," he replied, with the familiar gesture of rubbing his forefinger and thumb together. "It takes money. It's a rich man's country of fine homes and broad acres, expensive restaurants and beautifully gowned women—a place where 'you are my honey, if you have money.' The poor are found at the end of muck sticks, or picks, burrowing tunnels through the mountains, while living in boxcars. Others are bindle stiffs, itinerants, picking fruit for a pittance. When they are too old to labor, you find them on a Poor Farm. It is no place for such as we," he concluded. "With limited education and without means, it is better for us here."

But the impression his talk made on me was as deep and lasting as the lines from Richard Stoddard's verse:

> If in youth, the dream departs,
> It takes something from our hearts
> And it never comes again.

California, once a distant dream for me, now came into focus. To realize my ambition to go there, when would I be better equipped than now?

The next Sunday morning I saddled Blaze and set out for home, intending to tell the family about my plans. I was sure there would be opposition and disappointment, and to counter it, I had rehearsed my lines well: "You would go, Pa, if you were I. You left the old country when you were eighteen, never to return—never again to see your mother, brother, or sister. I promise to return someday for a visit. Of course, right now, I can't say how soon that will be."

However, Pa did not offer the expected objection. He looked off into the distance, reminiscing perhaps on his own youth or his trip west. Ma looked at him pleadingly, wishing he might deter me. Finally Pa said, "Someday we will go there, too."

That afternoon, before returning to the Sweet Spring Ranch to finish the month, I made up an order to Sears, Roebuck for some clothes. It was a very small order, for I needed to conserve the little money I had.

Mr. Oates, disabled with his broken leg, did not accept lightly my notice of leaving. "I have some work that requires an experienced hand—a job that Mike can't do. Get on up to the north ranch," he ordered. "Cut out a bunch of fresh cows—cows with calves—to be broken for milking." Oates had planned on readying several strings to sell to the homesteaders and was determined not to miss the opportunity to supply their need.

Milking itself I considered degrading enough, but breaking half-wild prairie cows to milk was really at the bottom of my list. Those skinny long-legged range animals, when separated from their bawling calves, are mean and can be dangerous. Each one had to be roped and snubbed twice a day. It was incredible how they could kick even with their legs tied. The pail and I were sent rolling so often I always seemed to be saturated with milk. At first I got scarcely enough to feed the half-starved calves. They butted both me and the pail before I could get my fingers in their mouths, the first step in teaching them to drink. Such mishaps, along with the continued intermittent ghostly noises at my cabin, added to my joyful anticipation of leaving, and I looked forward to the last day of October.

I tried either to ignore or to sleep through most of the ghostly visits, and the dog named Pancake which slept beside my cot helped some. I wondered why I had not thought of him before. He seemed to fear nothing, and with him a person could feel safe even in the corral with the big red bull, for he kept the bull's attention fully occupied. Parrying the bull's charges, Pancake would manage to get a toothhold on his nose and hold on until the bull ran off bawling. He was a mixed breed of unknown lineage and had acquired his name by always being around at breakfast time displaying his penchant for pancakes.

Pancake slept peacefully and I was not disturbed by noises until the second night before leaving. Along with hard rain, a storm brought terrific thunder, lightning, and high winds with eerie and unusual sounds. There was a sound unmistakably that of a horse pounding and splashing through mud and water in great haste. When it came to a sudden stop, I heard footsteps almost immediately on the stairs. Had the rider dismounted, and was he, she, or it ascending my stairway? Pancake scurried toward the screen door barking furiously. I was right behind him and peered out but neither saw nor heard anything other than shadows revealed by the flashes of lightning.

Pancake returned to his post and remained tense, his head resting on his paws pointed toward the door. I dozed off, only to be awakened by a shrill scream coming from the direction of the house. The storm had ceased, and the moon shone brightly through a few clouds. As I jumped to my feet and rushed to the door, there were more screams, frightened and terrified. The flickering light of a candle and then a lamp appeared in an upstairs window. Tremulous sobbing continued while shadows moved about and voices attempted to soothe: "It won't get you—

it won't hurt you. Nothing there, nothing to be afraid of—Mommy and Daddy are here." After repeated assurances, the sobbing lessened and finally ceased. All was quiet, but the lamp remained lighted throughout the rest of the night.

Neither of the Oates boys went to school the next day. When I saw Harry in the yard, I walked over. "Hello, Harry," I greeted him, friendly like, hoping he might enlighten me, but he appeared frightened and made for the house.

Later in the day I sought still another opportunity to learn what had happened during the night. When, as usual, I saddled Willie's pony, I tried not to appear unnecessarily inquisitive in asking the younger boy: "Did you hear anything last night?"

"Sure did," he replied. "That was Harry. He gets moonstruck. When he sees things, he stands up in bed and screams his head off. He really sees 'em, too."

I did not press him further, although I had gained no satisfaction. What he had said seemed only to verify a ghostly apparition and added to my discomfort and annoyance. In all the stories of ghosts and strange phenomena I had ever read or heard, there was always a reasonable explanation. Surely this experience was not an exception, and I decided to use every means to bring this mystery into the open, although I had little time left to do so. Search as I did that day I could find nothing, and the following day, my last day of work, was my final opportunity to discover the source of the ghostly sounds—and appearances.

Several times I had already moved everything movable around the outside of the cabin—a bench on which there was a washbasin, a couple boards, a set of hames that hung on a nail, a scythe, and other things of little consequence. Inside the cabin I had either moved or checked everything and searched every corner. Willie's report of Harry's seeing something caused me to consider extending my search beyond the cabin, but in sheer desperation I decided I would first look through the cabin again. Inside were a few pieces of old furniture, a humpbacked leather trunk, pieces of farm equipment, a dress form, a rococo-framed faded picture of a woman, and many other things, but nothing that when disturbed would emit any sound.

Closing the door when leaving, I thought I heard a thump, and opened it but there was nothing. Again I closed the door, and again heard a sound, like footsteps behind me. I tried the door again and closed it with the same result. Did the sound come from within or without? I wasn't sure. I went in, this time closing the door. The sound was more distinct and seemed to come from outside.

Investigating outside again, I came to an old mirror attached to the wall just above the bench and washbasin. I had failed to remove it in my search, but since it was almost flush with the boards on which it hung I figured it could not possibly cause any sounds. I was so jittery the sight of an image in the mirror startled me. I soon realized it was my own reflection, but with almost two weeks growth of beard, it was enough to startle any-one. I then realized that although I stood still, the mirror and the image in it seemed to move. Removing it carefully from the rusty nail, I discovered a triangular hole where a piece of board had broken off. Holding my hand over the hole, I felt a rush of air. Encouraged, I continued my scrutiny and found that the wind entered the cabin through an open window on the other side and funneled through that small opening and caused the mirror to bump. The sound, scarcely audible from the out-side of the cabin, was distinct inside, and especially so in the still of night. In the daytime and often at night the cabin door was open so the wind escaped through it; that explained why I had never heard the sound in daytime.

I replaced the mirror and closed the cabin door. With the next gust of wind, there it was, "bump . . . bump," loudly at first, just like someone coming up the stairs, then more rapidly but not quite so loud as the corners of the mirror struck alter-nately, simulating footsteps running down, and stopped until another gust of wind started it into motion again.

Eureka! This was my ghost! "Wahoo!" I shouted and tossed the mirror into the air. How good it was that I could leave for California with the mystery of the ghost behind me. I had to tell someone and rushed down to the barn.

"Mike, Mike," I shouted as soon as I saw him, "I found the ghost!"

He looked at me wide-eyed, his mouth agape.

"No fooling!" I continued when I drew near him. "I really did!"

"What—where?" he stammered.

"In the cabin," I announced. "He comes out at night, through a knothole."

Mike was speechless and swallowed hard. Visibly shaken, he waited for me to continue. It would have been cruel to keep him in suspense. As soon as I had explained everything—the mirror, the wind, the hole in the wall—I said, "Now you can go back to your old bunk in the cabin. In fact, if you prefer, you can even have mine!"

"Gee, thanks," he said, with a sigh of relief.

"You know, I finally took Pancake up there with me," I told him, and we laughed over my experiences. "Remember the storm we had?" I continued. "That night I even imagined I heard a horseman galloping and splashing through mud."

"That really was a horse," Mike interrupted. "One broke loose at the north ranch. All that thunder and lightning must have frightened him. Anyway, he sure made for the home barn. Came in fast, dragging his rope. I got up and got him settled."

It was my turn to be relieved. "Oh, by the way, Mike," I added, "if you ever hear any screams in the night, that will be Harry, and nothing to worry about—he gets moonstruck and sees things."

Since the curse of the ghost and the phantom rider had ended happily and I was still curious about Harry's nightmares, I decided to try to learn a little more about his outbursts when Willie came along to have me saddle his pony for the final time. I had hoped to find out the cause and what Harry actually saw, but Willie continued only to insist they were caused by the moon and that "Harry really and truly sees things!"

My final day of work arrived at last. The wonders of California seemed just beyond the horizon whereas only a few short weeks before they had been a million miles away. California meant the end of stinking stables, corrals that reeked of sweat and dung, and barns that smelled of rope and leather. My hands, encrusted with calluses deforming them into claws, would heal eventually. In California there would be no frosted feet, no lungs seared by the cold. I dreamed of fruits and flowers, of orchards and vineyards, of lofty mountains reflected in a blue ocean.

Morning came on the song of the meadowlark, the sun spilling over the horizon to flood the plains with light. Out in the corral the calves were bawling, setting up a din, waiting to be fed, but my job had been concluded the evening before. In another corral the cows were milling around stirring up clouds of dust and Mike was having all kinds of trouble, getting tangled in the rope, burning his hands. Bess stood by, holding a milk pail. As a tribute to her kindness, I took the pail from her and did the milking. She showed her appreciation by preparing a wonderful breakfast of pancakes, sausage, eggs, and canned peaches, following which Mr. Oates paid me off, grumbling.

Scrubbed, shaved, and in clean clothes, I started for the horse corral, saddle on my shoulder, bridle in my hand. When Blaze saw me, he circled around, tossing his head and pawing the ground. As I opened the gate, he snorted and charged out, tail high, as though to run away. He didn't go far before coming to an abrupt stop. Circling around in a wide turn at an even trot, he came back to nuzzle at the pocket in which I kept his sugar. He accepted the bit eagerly, indicating impatience while I cinched the saddle and secured my blanket roll. Little did he know we were about to make our last ride together.

Riding by the gate, I waved a cheery good-bye. Mr. Oates, on the porch, waved his cane angrily. "You're not worth your salt!" he called after me. "You're no damn good!" He shouted as though attempting to be heard in the next county: "If you were half a man, you would have stayed the season out!" Bess, behind him, gave a discreet wave and smiled.

I rode out and away from the ranch, too happy to care about anything.

A TIME OF DECISION

WITH A SENSE OF FREEDOM I rode down the road. The wide expanse of prairie was a wonderful place to be—it was all mine that gorgeous autumn morning. The fact that it was Sunday added to the peace and quiet that was everywhere. High white clouds moved almost imperceptibly in a pale blue sky as cattle lay in the warming sun that followed the chill of the late October night. I passed a cornfield surrounded by a strong fence and noted the leaves had turned to a green gold but the crop had not dried enough to husk.

At Gannvalley I took a preplanned detour. Turning off toward the northwest, I followed the familiar road leading to the Saunders Ranch. There was not a soul in sight on the road as far as I could see; in fact there was no sign of movement anywhere except for an occasional little dust devil swirling on the road or a hawk circling lazily in the sky. At such times I customarily played the harmonica I always carried in my saddle pocket. I liked the popular songs that expressed sweet sorrow: "Farewell My Blue Belle," "Red River Valley," "Red Wing," "Bury Me Not on the Lone Prairie," and "The Cowboy's Dream," as well as others. On still days such as this, the sound of music was gloriously magnified. Blaze, lifting his feet high like a show horse on parade, kept pace with it.

At the creek bend where water and road almost merge, two ponies grazed while two little boys sat nearby fishing under low trees.

"Have any luck?" I asked.

"One," the nearer boy quickly responded.

"We just got here," the other one said, as if in apology.

The smaller of the boys, a freckle-faced lad with missing front teeth, held up the wriggling prize. "You heading for the Saunders place?" he asked.

"They're not home," he replied in answer to my nod. "No one. We just came through."

"Do you know them?" I asked.

"Sure," they spoke in unison. "Miss Saunders is our new teacher."

News of Sis teaching was a surprise to me. I asked the obvious: "Do you like her?"

"Yes, she's real nice," the older boy answered.

"She's thwell!" the younger one exclaimed through his missing teeth.

Like many other lonesome ranch lads, the boys wanted to prolong the conversation. "Nice horse you have. What's his name?"

"Blaze," I answered, patting his hide gently. Blaze sensed he was being admired.

"What do you know? Mine is Firefly—we call him Fly. His is George."

"George! Now, that's a nice name for a horse," I said. "That's my name."

"I'm Artie," the older boy said. "Artie Springer. He's Emil Schiesow." I did not find that name so unusual as he had expected, for I had met the boy's father.

"We'll see Miss Saunders tomorrow. Can we tell her anything for you?" Artie offered as I turned Blaze to leave.

"You may tell her George came to say good-bye," I replied, disappointed that Sis was not home, for now I could never try to narrow the moat between me and the ivory tower in which dwelt the little princess—as I envisioned our stations. I had intended this meeting to be my moment of triumph, yet she might have accepted my news as unimportant. In that event, her absence from home would have been for the best.

I continued on to the ranch, feeling not all was lost, for the ride was enjoyable and I had longed to see again the ranch that would forever have a place in my heart. Knowing no one was there to greet me, I stopped atop the rise beyond where the hay road crossed the creek and looked over the familiar sights: pigeons on the roof of the big red barn, the windmill that groaned and clanked when turned on each morning to whir throughout the day, cool clear water splashing into the huge tank, and guinea hens reminding me of their raucous cacophony each morning arousing me to my daily chores. Laundry hung on the line which meant that Elsa had washed out a few things— undergarments, no doubt, which she first enclosed in pillow cases before hanging so they were out of sight.

Sydney, the longhaired Australian sheep dog, came slowly up the road, peering through the long hair over his eyes, barking for attention until I got down to pet him. I remounted Blaze and reluctantly continued my journey toward home. I had not gone far when a horse came into view. It was being led and was coming in my direction. My heart leaped higher than a meadow-lark's song when I became aware it was Sis leading Molly.

"I'm a mess," she said as I rode up, her lips pursed forming dimples in her pretty cheeks.

"You look awfully sweet to me," I said, "even with your torn stocking and dust all over you. Did you get piled?"

"You could call it that," she replied. "Molly stepped into a badger hole. Neither of us saw it; we were so intent on driving the cattle away from the haystacks."

Dismounting, I placed an arm around her shoulder and examined the bruise on her elbow. "Hurt?" I asked.

"No, not really," she replied.

There was a trickle of blood on Molly's knee, so Sis trotted the mare around until she satisfied herself there was no lameness. We sat down on a large flat rock among many smaller ones along the side of the road, and I prepared to tell her of my imminent departure, but she beat me to it and spoke first.

"This is rather a lucky day," she began. "I'm sure glad you came by. I have some news for you I hope you'll like."

About her school, I thought, but I would let her tell it and not let on I already knew she was teaching. "I have news for you, too," I said, but she seemed not to hear.

Instead her eyes lit up as though with a sudden bright idea. "Let's ride over to the Little Lake," she said.

This was more than I could ever have expected. I accepted her suggestion eagerly. The Little Lake! I had absorbed some of the feeling Fanny had for it through the stories she told me of her childhood there and how it had been held a charmed and sacred spot by the Indians.

We were approximately seven miles from the lake and hurried toward it, trotting the horses, holding hands. In less than a half hour we reached Sy and Fanny's place. I was disappointed to see the extent of deterioration that had taken place in such a short time. Boards on the little cabin that had never known paint were loose, the rusted tin chimney was held at a crazy angle by a strand of barbed wire, and the water barrel staves had parted and stood among the loosened hoops.

"Let's stop here a minute. I want to look inside," I told Sis and dismounted. Sis could not possibly know the thoughts that came to me on what was to be my last visit to this site, my first "home away from home." She sat her mount waiting to go on.

Although the door stood ajar, I walked around to peer through the little window of the lean-to. It looked about the same as when I had last seen it. My cot still stood against the wall, and I shuddered remembering the terrifying night Sy had come home drunk, accusing Fanny of infidelity and threatening repeatedly to slit my throat from ear to ear.

In the barnyard, the two flat-roofed animal shelters that had been formed of Indian poles had caved in. Fanny's garden in which she had labored so hard was overgrown with weeds. Broken and rusted pieces of farm equipment that had already passed their prime when Sy acquired them lay strewn about, along with bits of old harness and some of Fanny's old shoes. I found the plow, recalling my initiation to full days of toil, remembering also the first happy hours of seeing the shining, black, sweet-smelling earth roll over the moldboard to form long unbroken ribbons while sea gulls flew gracefully about searching for fat white grubs.

I did not want to keep Sis waiting longer and remounted

Blaze. At a fast trot we crossed the field I once plowed, which was now covered with gray brown weeds and returning to prairie, through what had been the pasture, and down across the meadow where the grass, now cut, grew lush.

The lake lay calm except for the ripples made by water trickling over the rocks. Never could it have looked more inviting, more beautiful. From the meadow I gathered armloads of hay which I tossed over the fence before following Sis along her secret path hidden by willows and chokecherry bushes.

"There is no need for that fence," she said. "I am going to ask Daddy to have it taken down." I noted that she had begun referring to her father as Daddy. We spread the sweet-smelling hay under the trees where I had once gotten a glimpse of her lying in the sun while shadows of plum blossoms formed patterns of pink and gray over her body.

A whisper of breeze stirred brilliant colored leaves from the trees to drift in the limpid water. Swallows darted in and out from under the clay bank, and dragonflies flashed blue on translucent wings—"devil's darning needles" Sis called them, reminiscent of her childhood. White butterflies darted to rest on the bronze red wild plums. Neither of us mentioned Fanny, but I could hear the Indian girl, as though she were by my shoulder, eyes shining and smiling, talking of her now-lost dream: "Someday I will build my house there."

We didn't talk much, our conversation mainly monosyllables, sweet and soft, slow and lazy. I was forever awed by the changes in Sis after having not seen her for a while. Maturity added to her beauty and self-assurance and made me feel awkward and clumsy, not knowing just what she expected of me. I kept pushing my too-long hair back from over my eyes. "I had planned on getting it cut in Kimball," I told her and checked myself, deciding not to add "before I leave."

I brightened when she suggested we take off our shoes and stockings to wade out into the water. We crossed over to the other side where she knew of a comfortable seat formed of field stones partially obscured by the wash of sand and soil. There was an overhang of grass that dipped into the water where we sat dangling our feet, hers looking childlike beside mine. Her legs were a creamy softness in contrast to the lovely tan of her face and arms.

Down at the shallow end, ducks chattered to each other softly among the reeds. A mallard drake, with a gleaming green head and a curl of feathers over his tail, came slowly toward us to scold before turning away, leaving wavelets forming a wedge in his wake. The hen mallard, almost the color of Blaze, circled about nervously.

Grebes, the little "hell divers," were more venturesome because of their ability to turn tail up and disappear at any moment. Where they would come up moments later one could not foretell —one here, another there, soundless and as though from out of nowhere, they appeared and again swam about peacefully and unconcerned.

An old cottonwood tree off to the side, its roots protruding where the bank had washed away, was making a valiant and apparently successful effort to survive, its top broken off, probably by a storm. New bark which replaced some that had been torn off proved to be an ideal place in which to carve our initials, each enclosed by an interlocking heart. I drove the knife deep, hoping the symbol would remain for Sis to view and remember for many years.

The carving finished, I stood back to admire my handiwork. "G.B. loves S.S.," I said before turning where Sis could see the warm blush that had come to my cheeks.

"S.S. loves G.B.," she countered with more self-assurance as she put her arms tightly around my waist. Then she teasingly pulled out my shirttail and ran off anticipating I would try to catch her, which wasn't too difficult. I carried her out into the water threatening to dunk her, clothes and all, enjoying her squeals. Her arms grew tighter around my neck as I lowered her as far as I dared without getting her wet.

Once again seated beside me on the sweet-smelling hay, she dried her feet with my new bandana before putting on her long, black ribbed cotton stockings and shoes.

"I've waited long for a moment like this," I said and folded her close in my arms. Her response was warm.

"There will be more such moments, many more. When you get home, you'll find a letter—from Daddy—asking you to come to work for us."

It was hard for me to believe—especially coming as it did at this time.

"Yes," she continued, with delightful animation, "you will be in charge, even more so after Mother and Daddy leave for Europe. That will be after the cattle are shipped."

This unexpected turn of events left me almost speechless.

"What about you?" I asked. "You're not going with them?"

"Oh! You don't know, do you? I'm teaching." She misunderstood my hesitation. "If you are concerned about me, you needn't be," she said mischievously. "Elsa is stricter than either Mother or Daddy."

Anything I could say after that seemed anticlimactic. "Honey," I finally said after a long pause, "that makes it hard to tell you. I'm going to California."

She looked at me with deep hurt and disbelief. "When?" she asked.

"Tomorrow," I replied. "I'm on my way home. Came around this way to tell you and to say good-bye."

"Why didn't you let me know before?" she asked.

"Because I didn't even know it myself," I told her. "I hadn't given it a thought until after Al left for Texas. Besides, I didn't think you would care."

"Care?" she exclaimed. "Of course, I do—ever since you were at Sy's. I was happy when you came to live at our place. Daddy thought we were too young then to be seeing each other so much, but two years have made a difference. And what about the years to come?"

"That's what I've been thinking of. I can't settle for a job as a ranch hand or even a foreman," I said frankly.

She began, as if to say something, but hesitated, seeming to change her mind. "Do you really want to go?" she asked in a questioning sort of disbelief.

"No, not really," I answered, "but I must, if I'm to make any sort of life for myself."

Her disappointment began to reveal itself. "And you couldn't do that here?" she asked, as tears began to rim her eyes. I felt the dampness on my face when I held her close. Where now was the moat, the ivory tower, that moment of triumph that now I did not want?

Neither of us said anything. We lay back on the hay, in the warmth of the sun, oblivious to the things around us; our world was only each other. She closed her eyes as I gazed upon each beautiful feature of her face. Her long brown eyelashes lay against her cheeks, lightly dusted over with summer freckles. Soft waves of curls wound about her neck and came to rest under her chin. Her dress, a charming one I knew she had made herself, lay softly over the perfect contours of her body. I thought that a time like this should last forever, but the sun continued to move, and all too soon it began to get low in the sky.

Time came when we had to part, at least for the day, for by then I was sure I did not want to go away.

"I have to go now," she said—once, twice, and then again, with more emphasis, squeezing my arms with her slender but firm hands. Just as I was sure I did not want to go away, she seemed to be even more certain that I wouldn't.

"You don't want to go," she said, looking into my eyes. "I don't want you to." She kissed me softly on the lips. "Don't go," she urged. "Call for me at the school. I'll be waiting for you." As though to make it final, she broke away and ran, taking quick little steps around the lake to skip over rocks in the shallows, hurrying on through the willows and berry brush.

With scarcely the touch of the stirrup, she gained her mount and was away, giving no backward glance until coming to the long dip in the road where she reined up, gave a hearty wave, and disappeared from sight.

The spell that had enveloped us throughout that golden afternoon lingered on. Alone with my thoughts, I tried to relive some of its precious moments: how Sis looked and the things she had said. When she declared, "I must have that fence taken down," had her thoughts projected beyond to a future cottage on the site—perhaps white with green shutters—a common thought among young women of marriageable age. "Two years made a difference," she had said, and I reflected that it had, in each of us. "There is something fine in physical labor and callused hands," she had said, when I offered an apology for the roughness of mine, and she placed them to her cheek. "We will read to each other and study together," held a wonderful promise for the coming long and cold winter evenings not far off now. There followed no word, no further thought of parting. California seemed long since to have been forgotten as though it had never been thought of at all.

The sun had already touched the brim of the horizon when I came out of my reverie. The sides of the haystacks to the west caught and reflected its last golden rays; the sides toward the east were gray, the shadows long.

"Blaze, old fellow," I said as I turned his nose toward home, "we have a lot of thinking to do, and the time is short."

I approached our farm the long way around by the section

lines. When the house came into view, a light was burning in the window. They had expected me earlier for what was intended to be my one last day at home.

VISTAS

I DID NOT LEAVE on the following day or on the day after that. I was in deep torment, burdened with a secret I could not share and a decision I could not make. The family interpreted my morose silence as due solely to the contents of Mr. Saunders's letter, which I had found waiting unopened on the kitchen table.

"What can this be?" I said, pretending surprise and giving no indication I already knew its message, for telling about meeting Sis would have destroyed the glamour of an afternoon I felt belonged to us alone. Glancing over Mr. Saunders's neatly handwritten page, I commented, "It's a job offer," and read the cordial, businesslike letter aloud.

A faint glimmer of hope sparkled in Ma's eyes. Although she was resigned to my leaving, I knew she did not favor it.

Pa suggested, "Home here isn't so bad, after all. Perhaps you better consider taking that job."

"It is a big temptation," I said slowly, not giving any hint as to the real reason.

I did not sleep much that night, and Monday my mind continued to wrestle with the problem. Several friends had heard I was leaving and telephoned to say good-bye. Each envied me, or so they said, and their good wishes raised my spirits.

After supper I rode over to visit the Balsters. Nora and I had always had a sort of camaraderie, and I knew she would be a comfort, for to her nothing was ever of momentous importance. She had always seemed mature beyond her years. She greeted me at the door with, "I'm so happy you came over," speaking in her usual low voice, her modest reserve permitting a faint smile.

"So you're really going to California," she began as we

seated ourselves in the comfortable living room. "Do you think you'll stay?"

"Well, I hope to," I managed to say rather convincingly, although I was still wavering in my decision to leave.

"Gus Galkey was disappointed there. He couldn't get steady work," Nora continued. "Many Chinese and Mexicans make for cheap labor, and much of the state is either mountainous or desert, not suited for farming and cattle." She agreed with me, however, that there were many advantages.

"Oh, I have something for you," she announced, going to the piano, "but don't expect California to be this beautiful." She held up the colorful sheet music for the current hit song, "Where the Sunset Turns the Ocean's Blue to Gold." Her three equally lovely brown-eyed sisters gathered around the piano joining us in the song we would henceforth associate with each other.

It was past the Balsters' bedtime when I left at nine-thirty. As we said good-bye, Nora confided that she had been doing some fancy stitching: "I've been working on something for you, a little gift. If it isn't finished before you leave, I'll mail it."

The following morning after Ed and Agnes had gone to school, I was sitting at the kitchen window watching Nick repair the corncribs and gazing aimlessly over the dry prairie when a team of horses and a spring wagon came into view. Since it was arriving from the Balsters' direction and the lines were held high, one in each hand, sufficient evidence that the driver was a woman, I exclaimed, "Here comes Nora!"

"Where?" Ma asked, flustered and startled.

"Across the prairie," I answered.

"Is she coming here?" Ma's voice was anxious.

"Where else?" I quipped.

"Mercy! Goodness!" Since no company ever came to our house, Ma was totally unprepared and rushed outside immediately to bring in the wet wash from the line: patched overalls, underwear made of Klietsch and Halmes' White Lily flour sacks, and my torn and faded baseball uniform with the elastic gone and now being used as underwear.

Pa shaved hurriedly, changed into a clean shirt, and put on his best pants that now hung loosely on his once corpulent frame, the result of less accessible beer. Ma might have laughed at the way his pants sagged at the rear had she not been so busy trying to tidy the one room that served as our living room, dining room, and kitchen. Our home was no match for the Balsters'; but Ma really did not need to concern herself, for neither was anyone else's in the township.

"I suppose you'll have to bring her in here," Ma sighed as Nora drove up.

Nora was dressed prim and proper, as usual. Her dark wool skirt was ankle length, and her blue print silk shirtwaist with a Peter Pan collar was immaculate and becoming. Her black hair, neatly drawn back to a bun, was waved at the front into a pompadour. I was flattered to see that she was wearing a locket in which there was a picture of me that she had cut from a snapshot.

"I brought you the little gift I mentioned last night. I sat up and finished it," she said, handing me two white linen handkerchiefs on which she had embroidered my initials. "I also brought the camera," she continued. "Since it's such a beautiful day, I thought we could take some pictures."

"Of course, how thoughtful," Ma said, smiling as Nora opened the folding camera. "I wish my asters were still blooming. They'd have been a nice setting." She looked around for another background to suggest, obviously relieved the picture taking would keep us outdoors.

Nora took my picture alone and in a group shot with Ma, Pa, and Nick. Afterwards, Nick took one of Nora and me standing arm in arm behind a clump of tansy. She was about to leave when, to Ma's dismay, Pa asked if she couldn't stay and have dinner with us. Nora, however, declined the invitation and said regretfully that she had to get back home. I rode beside her down the lane as far as the section line, where in our last good-bye there was no display of affection other than a friendly handshake. To Nora, a kiss would have been an eternal promise.

Pa was still in his best clothes and in the yard when I got back. *"Ein gnädiges fräulein,"* he commented. I turned and looked as Nora, the farm team, and the spring wagon slowly faded from our view. "Yes, a fine girl," I agreed, for Nora was certainly a gracious and charming person.

By that time I felt I had committed myself to California to the point where I could no longer turn back. I had acknowledged everyone's telephoned good-bye and had accepted Nora's parting gift. Perhaps it was for the best that I go ahead with my plans to leave, I reasoned, knowing the longer I stayed the harder it would be to leave. I decided to go the very next day, while my mind was made up.

I felt somewhat relieved after making the decision and began to pack my meager belongings—one extra pair of socks, a white shirt, a change of underwear, the handkerchiefs Nora had embroidered, and my shaving things. In one corner of my suitcase I put the Birdseye stove-matchbox which held my collection of arrowheads, snake rattles, and the agates I had found in Fanny's cache at the Little Lake. These items, in addition to the cheap mail-order clothing I would wear on the train, represented all of my worldly possessions after four years of hard and sometimes dangerous work. I owned no watch and no jewelry of any kind, but I did not feel poor. In those four years I had acquired strength and endurance which, along with youth, was more than anyone could buy.

When Ed got home from school, I gave him my cowboy hat, my scuffed and worn boots, and my spurs. "Oh, boy!" he shouted and strutted out to try his skill at roping calves before stowing the gear under his cot.

I could not bear the thought of actually giving away Blaze, the joy of my life, and preferred to think I was just turning him, his saddle, and bridle over to Nick. I was satisfied, for I knew that with Nick Blaze would have the best of care. I would never need to worry that my horse might fall into other hands.

If Nick was unhappy over my leaving, he failed to show it after acquiring Blaze. Beaming with pleasure, he talked cheerfully about taking me to the train and how he would at the same time sell a load of Ma's turkeys and take care of a few errands, which included purchasing a number of things he needed.

Ma's turkeys had gorged themselves all summer on the grasshoppers that riddle crops and cover fields and roads during dry years and were therefore fat as butterballs and ready for market. Ma was always glad to see Nick drive toward town with turkeys for she had been quite upset and angry about the coyotes which she complained "continue to cut down my turkey flock, in spite of their perching on top of the barns and sheds at night. Those coyotes are so sly, lying in wait to get my turkeys at the break of day. Nick has been able to get a shot at only one—and those turkeys have been so hard to raise." She was probably thinking of the many times she had taken young turkeys into the kitchen to dry each with a towel because they didn't have sense enough to seek shelter from the rain, and remembering too the ones that had fallen prey to hawks and rats.

On my last day at home we got up earlier than usual because of loading the turkeys. We had to be outside before dawn to get them down from their roof-perches before they had their eyes open. I said good-bye to Ed and Agnes before they left for school. Most of the morning, Ma busied herself in the kitchen preparing an extra good meal and packing a lunch for the long train ride that lay ahead of me. As the time to leave approached, the task of replying to Mr. Saunders's letter could be put off no longer. I wrote a short note to thank him and explained why I could not accept his offer. I started a letter to Sis but, after many erasures and changes, decided the message contained in my letter to her father would have to suffice.

No one said much during the early dinner. Nick was anxious to get started because of the turkeys and other business he had in town. He went to get the horses and had them hitched to the wagon and waiting when we came out. As we said good-bye, I sensed that Ma was determined not to show her disappointment at my decision. Pa's good-bye was short, Germanic in both word and character: *"Passen auf und auf Wiedersehen."*

Nick slapped the horses gently on their rumps. "Chk, chk, Ben, Cap," he called to them, "let's go." They had had a long season of hard work and moved slowly, as if hitched to a drag or a plow.

"Say good-bye again to Ed and Agnes for me," I called back. The wagon creaked down the lane edged with weeds. The cornfield on one side was mostly nubbins, suitable only as fodder; the other side of the lane had a rusted and useless barbed wire fence, its broken parts leaning crazily this way and that.

At the end of the lane where the road cut across the prairie, I turned for a last look at the shabby house made of lean-tos on the bare windswept knoll and the big weatherbeaten barn with its sway-backed roof. I expected never to see the farm again. Pa, appearing to be busy with a shovel on his shoulder, had begun to walk slowly toward the potato patch at the back of the house. Ma, clutching the corner of her apron in one hand, was waving to me.

The wagon bumped over the rock-strewn rutted road with its washed out depressions. The sky was slightly overcast and a cool breeze flowed over the roll of prairie, the first warning of winter. Nick rolled down the sleeves of his hickory shirt over his muscular forearms and buttoned the collar. "Won't be long now before snow flies," he said, looking up at a flock of geese that honked overhead on their way south. "Can look for snow flurries any day," he continued. I visualized the fields and roads under a mantle of white, glad that I would not have to contend with that kind of winter this year.

Nick remained strangely silent during most of the long slow ride, the reins hanging loosely in his bronzed and callused hands. At one point he said, "I wish I were going with you," knowing the futility of his statement. His remark surprised me, for I had not thought Nick might also want to get away.

"But how would the rest of the family get along if I left?" he continued. "I have to stay."

"They couldn't make it without you," I agreed. "I wonder if Pa realizes it. Perhaps I shouldn't be traipsing off, but someday I'll make it up to you somehow."

"Aw, you don't need to feel that way. You don't owe anyone anything—you've done your share. I'm glad for you, glad you're going to have a chance."

When we reached Kimball, Nick dropped me off at the barber's. "I'll meet you at Gus Sobek's," he said, as he drove off to sell the turkeys and take care of his errands: a stop at Whitbeck and Lombard Bank, a few purchases for the family, and some farm supplies at Brooks Hardware and Lumber Yard.

The saloon was the customary and respectable place for men to meet. Gus Sobek, Big's brother, was from out our way. "So you're going to California," he offered when I walked in. "Well, I'll be doggone! Wish I was goin' with ya, but I got three brothers and three sisters here—wouldn't want to leave 'em. My youngest brother, Joe, though—he'll go there someday, 'at's about all he talks about."

Tony Kovanda and Ed Pitsek came in, and Gus said, "Whaddaya know, George here's goin' to California."

"Well, I'll be!" Tony exclaimed, turning to Ed. "This calls for a celebration to send him off." Each wanted to buy me a drink, and so did Fred Runge, who came in just after they left, followed shortly by Nick. I had three or four Virginia Dares. (I didn't really care for Virginia Dares, but I had to be sociable and they weren't very potent.)

Fred Runge, Gus and Tador's brother, decided that since we

were such good friends and not likely to have another opportunity soon we should have our picture taken together—Gus, Nick, Fred, and I. After that was accomplished, it was time for Nick to start back to get over the prairie road before dark. "Sorry I can't stay with you until train time," he said.

I said good-bye to Fred and watched Nick drive down the dirt street, then I went back inside, for Gus had invited me to stay for supper with him in the kitchen at the back of his saloon.

"How does a nice thick steak sound to you?" Gus asked me. "You've been around a lot of beef on the hoof out there, but I bet ya didn't get fresh meat very often."

"Only in the winter," I agreed, "and sometimes when I got into town. Steak sounds great."

Gus left a bottle and glasses on the bar for his regular customers to pour their own, and some of them looked in for a short visit afterwards. By the time we finished supper and washed the dishes, train time was near. Gus handed me a bottle of Old Crow and a handful of cigars. "Here, take these with you." I felt flattered by his kindness toward me.

When I stepped out into the gray dusk, the street was deserted, with no horses at the hitching poles. To the west, the sky was outlined in ragged streaks of orange. A light appeared over the door of the Kimball House, in expectation of a possible guest arriving on the incoming train. Lights were coming on here and there, including a dim glow at the railroad station as I made my way toward it.

The train would stop for only a moment, just long enough for an exchange of mail and some freight or baggage and for passengers to board. That evening I was apparently the only one who was catching the train. In my pocket was the still unsealed letter for Mr. Saunders. By the dim light in the waiting room, I read it once again. How poorly written for Sis to see, I thought, and how cold the message she would share with her father. I hoped she would understand. Outside, the baggage cart with two milk cans and a couple of large boxes had already been moved into loading position.

The train was on time. As I heard its first whistle, I sealed the envelope and dropped the letter into the box. I didn't want it to be a last good-bye to Sis and decided I would write to her from California. The train roared in and I felt the quake of the little station.

"ALL A-BOARD!" cried the conductor in an authoritative

voice, as I mounted the steps and entered the car. The bell sounded immediately, an urgent clang followed by labored puffs of black smoke, the grating of wheels turning slowly, and the hiss of escaping steam. The train began to roll. A half-mile farther at the cattle guards and the crossing where the wagon road leads toward home, the whistle screeched its warning whoo-wa, whoo-a— a long, a short, a long. As the train picked up speed, Sis's words began to ring in my ears. "You will be leaving those who love you—those you love," seemed to be repeating over and over to the rhythmic clickety-clack, clickety-clack, clickety-clack of the wheels pounding and rolling over the rails.

Night fell over the prairie. I sat alone, my head turned to the window. Out in the blackness there was nothing to be seen but a single star.

EPILOGUE

❖

ALONE IN THE CITY

I EXPECTED NO HELP from Ma's relatives nor did I want it for I had come to California with the expectation I could make my own way. A few days after my arrival, only because I had promised Ma, I made the trip from the temporary cheap room I had rented to their home. Although my reception was cordial, it was far from warm, and they offered no advice or assistance. I now knew I could proceed on my own, as I had intended.

My first year was full of new and exciting experiences, but I learned the meaning of being friendless and jobless in a strange area. I soon discovered I was ill-clothed for the damp, wet chill and the relentless drizzle of the northern California winter as I looked for work in the big city—walking, walking, walking, from early morning until the dark of evening. I had decided that the Oakland side of the Bay had more opportunities for work for me than I would be likely to find in San Francisco. My route in Oakland took me along the waterfront where brackish water slapped against encrusted piles and dock workers handled the cargo of great ships, to the shipyards and dry docks and the rumble of huge cranes, to the factory section filled with smoke and acrid smells, and into the railroad yards with the constant noise and confusion of shunting cars. Work seemed to be in abundance for some, but there was none for me. It was the slack season of the year, and everywhere men shuffled along aimlessly—men without skills or references, unwanted and alone—I was one of them.

Even the immigrant had friends who had preceded him and

a section of town or a ghetto he could call home. From a young man cocky and full of confidence I was quickly reduced to what I was—an awkward rustic, dressed in cheap, ill-fitting mail-order clothes I did not know how to wear. Many names of streets and towns were of Spanish origin, and these I always mispronounced. I was out of place also at my boarding house where the dining tables were draped with white linen, people wore their Sunday-best for everyday, and men were always jacketed. Supper was not family style, the served plates were placed before us, usually beginning with a small salad—macaroni, or apple, known as a Waldorf or some such fancy name. Such strange things as artichokes I knew not how to eat, and they were far from filling. No dinner was served at noon, and breakfast was small, consisting of one egg, a little toast, and half an orange, plus coffee. There was never enough, but the boarders did not complain and never asked for more. The bar of soap in the washroom was hard as a horse's hoof. I learned later it was only for show and that one was expected to furnish his own. The gas jet was set to allow a bare minimum of light, while the Chinese sulphur matches, a thousand in a two-inch block, threw off such fumes as to assure their use only in emergencies. My first experience with indoor plumbing gave me the feeling of being immoral.

Nights were lonely, as my little store of money melted away, and my only diversion was a weekly visit to a five-cent Charlie Chaplin or Bill Hart movie, or to some poolroom where a man chewing on a cigar would ask, "Wanna stick?" meaning "Rent a cue or scram," or down to 7th Street where player pianos tinkled behind drawn shades, where the air was filled with the smell of hotdogs, onions, and hamburgers, and where girls of the evening prowled seductively.

Instinctively, I looked for familiar faces in every crowd. A nose, a mouth, or a walk would remind me of someone—I saw Sis as the mannequin in a store window or as the bride in white on the cover of a magazine. In my room I labored over letters to her, not knowing what to say. Then I always tore them up.

Moving from one place to another led to a small boarding-house in a poorer part of town. It was run by a widow, Hattie Dugan, who also did housework by the hour. She received assistance from her capable sixteen-year-old daughter Mickey who liked to be called "Michele."

It was a blustery March morning when, following Michele's suggestion, I walked rough terrain to Alameda Point where, although arriving early, I found a knot of perhaps twenty-five or thirty men at the S.P. car shops. Promptly at seven o'clock when the whistle blew, a man with a pockmarked face announced, "No hirings for the day."

The crowd parted dejectedly. A man past middle age wiped away some tears with the back of his palsied hands. The sight touched me deeply: to see a grown man cry! Would the lines in his face and his gnarled hands someday be my own?

For no reason at all, I stayed around, peering into the depth of the shops. Two men were plainly visible in a glassed-in office, on the door of which, in bold letters, was "Axel J. Orr, Superintendent." When one of the men, the younger of the two, stepped out, I made my entrance. "Mr. Orr," I began in a mixture of desperation and defiance, "I want a job."

The superintendent looked up, startled. "Mm-mm. Ever work around machinery?" he asked.

For the moment I cast aside Mickey's advice to say I was a native. "Yes, I worked on a grain separator in South Dakota," I replied, knowing full well that that wasn't the kind of machinery he had in mind.

"Oh?" he said, obviously pleased. "I'm from Minnesota, myself." He wrote something on a slip of paper which he then handed to me with "Take this to Mr. Feeney."

Mr. Feeney was the man with the pockmarked face. His reception was cool as he showed me to a machine, the likes of which I had never seen before. There I botched a few jobs; but since I was Mr. Orr's man, Feeney made no comment and I stayed on. It was my first steady job, seven days a week with time-and-a-half for Sundays.

During my first year in California, the letters from the family, still on the farm in South Dakota, were more infrequent than their trips to town. Nick was the correspondent: "Nothing much to write about except that it is proving to be a long cold winter and I am longing for spring when I can get out into the fields again."

When summer wore on, Nick's messages became discouraging: "We need rain. The ground is beginning to crack. The tender shoots of grain are curling up. . . . Hot dry winds—dust piled in drifts."

With crops failing and the experiences of drought and grasshoppers, Pa determined that it would be a good idea to sell out and bring the rest of the family to California, and everyone agreed. Their last year in South Dakota was a bad one, and they had a hard time disposing of their land at any price. After listing the place for sale, Pa became obsessed with moving to California although there were no buyers. He arranged to borrow and set a date for leaving, figuring a buyer for the land could be found later. Posters were out for an auction sale of the machinery, stock, and household goods. Nick's letter told me that the entire family would arrive in Oakland in ten days.

I was fearful at the thought of their coming, for they would expect me to help them, and I was a long way from being considered "established" and in no position to help them get located. Did they know that the S.P. shop had been closed? That my job was over? Did they know the difficulties I was having and the little help that I could give them? I wished they were arriving at a time when I was in better circumstances.

"Pa will find a small farm," Nick's letter stated. I shuddered when I read that. The farming situation in California was vastly different from that in South Dakota—could they adapt to conditions here? Did they know of the difficulties they were sure to encounter?

Fortunately before the family arrived, I again found work. I was one of the seven men at the Murray and Ready Employment Office, a place I had frequented myself in search of a few days' work. We were putting in full time, working on contract, sending railroad laborers by the hundreds to Klamath Falls and to the Rocklin-Colfax cutoff.

After greeting the family upon their arrival, I was not surprised that Pa's next act was the familiar rubbing of his thumb and forefinger together. Looking at the four five-dollar gold pieces I handed him, which was all the money I possessed, he asked, "Is that all you have?"

The family's first days in California were not too pleasant. Pa complained of the noise in the little hotel in which I had arranged for rooms, and he did not like the garlic in the Italian and Spanish food. They moved to a furnished house, which suited their needs while they looked for a desirable farm, finally deciding upon a twenty-two acre one near Hayward.

Nick had no trouble adjusting to farming in California. He conformed magnificently, and with the farm flourishing he was able to add more and more acres. Thus the farming venture that began in South Dakota became successful in California.

I had determined before leaving South Dakota that I had concluded my farm work, and the family's arrival did not alter my pattern of seeking to build a life for myself in the city. After many different jobs, and nights attending evening classes, I went to work at the age of twenty-three for a large New York insurance company. Advancement followed rapidly, and I knew finally I had achieved my goal of success.